ALSO BY H. P. BLAVATSKY:

The Secret Doctrine
An Invitation to The Secret Doctrine
The Key to Theosophy
The Voice of the Silence
Isis Unveiled
The Letters of H. P. Blavatsky to A. P. Sinnett
H. P. Blavatsky to the American Conventions: 1888–1891
From the Caves and Jungles of Hindostan
Gems from the East
Theosophical Glossary
Nightmare Tales
The People of the Blue Mountains
H. P. Blavatsky: Collected Writings I–XV

THEOSOPHICAL UNIVERSITY PRESS
PASADENA, CALIFORNIA

H. P. BLAVATSKY

SECRET DOCTRINE COMMENTARY

Stanzas I–IV

with a Section on Dreams

PHOTOGRAPHIC FACSIMILE EDITION

Transactions of the Blavatsky Lodge

THEOSOPHICAL UNIVERSITY PRESS
POST OFFICE BOX C
PASADENA, CALIFORNIA 91109–7107
1994

Originally published as *Transactions of the Blavatsky Lodge*
This reprint is an exact photographic facsimile in one volume of two booklets first issued in 1890 and 1891. No corrections have been made and nothing has been added to or omitted from the text. A new index has been included.

The paper in this book meets the standards for permanence and durability of the Council on Library Resources. ∞

Library of Congress Cataloging-in-Publication Data

Theosophical Society (Great Britain). Blavatsky Lodge.
    Secret doctrine commentary / stanzas I-IV : transactions of the Blavatsky Lodge / by H. P. Blavatsky.
    p.   cm.
    Originally published: Transactions of the Blavatsky Lodge of the Theosophical Society. London : Theosophical Publishing Society ; New York : W. Q. Judge, 1890–1891.
    Includes index.
    ISBN 1-55700-027-1 (alk. paper).
    ISBN 1-55700-028-x (alk. paper) pbk
    1. Blavatsky, H. P. (Helena Petrovna), 1831–1891. Secret doctrine. 2. Theosophy. I. Blavatsky, H. P. (Helena Petrovna), 1831–1891. II. Theosophical Society (Great Britain). Blavatsky Lodge. Transactions of the Blavatsky Lodge of the Theosophical Society. III. Title.
BP561.S4T433   1994
299′.934—dc20   94-7279
                                                                                    CIP

Printed at Theosophical University Press
Pasadena, California

TRANSACTIONS

OF

THE BLAVATSKY LODGE

OF THE

THEOSOPHICAL SOCIETY.

DISCUSSIONS ON THE STANZAS OF THE FIRST VOLUME

OF

THE SECRET DOCTRINE.

PART I.

STANZAS I AND II (SLOKAS I AND 2).

JANUARY, 1889.

London:
THE THEOSOPHICAL PUBLISHING SOCIETY,
7, DUKE STREET, ADELPHI, W.C.

New York:
W. Q. JUDGE, 132, NASSAU STREET
1890.

All Rights Reserved.

[*The following transactions are compiled from shorthand notes taken at the meetings of the Blavatsky Lodge of the Theosophical Society, from January 10th to June 20th, 1889, being somewhat condensed from the original discussions.*

" The Secret Doctrine" being based upon the archaic stanzas of the " Book of Dzyan," and these being too abstruse for most of the new students of Exoteric philosophy, the members of the " B. L. of the T. S." agreed to devote the debates of the weekly meetings to each stanza and sundry other metaphysical subjects.

The questions were put by members who, for the most part, supported their objections and exceptions on modern scientific grounds, and assumed logical deductions based thereon. As such objections are generally the common property of students of " The Secret Doctrine," it has been judged unnecessary to incorporate them in full, so that their substance alone has been retained. The answers in all cases are based on the shorthand Reports, and are those of Esoteric Philosophy as given by H P. B. herself.]

I.

Meeting held at 17, Lansdowne Road, London, W., on January 10th, 1889, at 8.30 p.m., MR. T. B. HARBOTTLE in the chair.

Subject:—

THE STANZAS OF THE SECRET DOCTRINE—VOL. I.

STANZA I.

Sloka (1). THE ETERNAL PARENT (*Space*), WRAPPED IN HER EVER INVISIBLE ROBES, HAD SLUMBERED ONCE AGAIN FOR SEVEN ETERNITIES.

Q. Space in the abstract is explained in the Proem (pp. 8 and 9) as follows :—

" . . . . Absolute unity cannot pass to infinity; for infinity presupposes the limitless extension of *something*, and the duration of that ' something '; and the One All is like Space—which is its only mental and physical representation on this Earth, or our plane of existence—neither an object of, nor a subject to, perception. If one could suppose the Eternal Infinite All, the Omnipresent Unity, instead of being in Eternity, becoming through periodical manifestation a manifold Universe, or a multiple personality, that Unity would cease to be one. Locke's idea that ' pure Space is capable of neither resistance nor motion ' is incorrect. Space is neither a ' limitless void ' nor a ' conditioned fulness,' but both, being on the plane of absolute abstraction, the ever-incognisable Deity, which is void only to finite minds, and on that of *mayavic* perception, the Plenum, the absolute Container of all that is, whether manifested or unmanifested; it is, therefore, that ABSOLUTE ALL. There is no difference between the Christian Apostle's ' In Him we live and move and have our being,' and the Hindu Rishi's, ' The Universe lives in, proceeds from, and will return to, Brahma (Brahmâ) '; for Brahma (neuter), the unmanifested, is that Universe *in abscondito*, and Brahmâ, the manifested, is the Logos, made male-female in the symbolical orthodox dogmas. The God of the Apostle-Initiate, and of the Rishi, being both the Unseen and the Visible SPACE. Space is called, in the esoteric symbolism, ' The Seven-Skinned Eternal Mother-Father.' It is composed from its undifferentiated to its differentiated surface of seven layers.

"' What is that which was, is, and will be, whether there is a Universe or not; whether there be gods or none ? ' asks the esoteric Senzar Catechism. And the answer made is—SPACE."*

---

* S. D., I., 8.

But why is the Eternal Parent, Space, spoken of as feminine?

A. Not in all cases, for in the above extract Space is called the "Eternal Mother-Father"; but when it is so spoken of the reason is that though it is impossible to define Parabrahm, yet once that we speak of that first something which *can* be conceived, it has to be treated of as a feminine principle. In all cosmogonies the first differentiation was considered feminine. It is Mulaprakriti which conceals or veils Parabrahm; Sephira the *light* that emanates first from Ain-Soph; and in Hesiod it is Gaea who springs from Chaos, preceding Eros (THEOG. IV.; 201—246). This is repeated in all subsequent and less abstract material creations, as witnessed by Eve, created from the rib of Adam, etc. It is the goddess and goddesses who come first. The first emanation becomes the immaculate Mother from whom proceed all the gods, or the anthropomorphized creative forces. We have to adopt the masculine or the feminine gender, for we cannot use the neuter *it*. From IT, strictly speaking, nothing can proceed, neither a radiation nor an emanation.

Q. *Is this first emanation identical with the Egyptian Neïth?*

A. In reality it is beyond Neïth, but in one sense or in a lower aspect it is Neïth.

Q. *Then the* IT *itself is not the "Seven-Skinned Eternal Mother-Father"?*

A. Assuredly not. The IT is, in the Hindu philosophy, Parabrahm, that which is beyond Brahmâ, or, as it is now called in Europe, the "unknowable." The space of which we speak is the female aspect of Brahmâ, the male. At the first flutter of differentiation, the Subjective proceeds to emanate, or fall, like a shadow into the Objective, and becomes what was called the Mother Goddess, from whom proceeds the Logos, the Son and Father God at the same time, both unmanifested, one the Potentiality, the other the Potency. But the former must not be confounded with the manifested Logos, also called the "Son" in all cosmogonies.

Q. *Is the first differentiation from the absolute* IT *always feminine?*

A. Only as a figure of speech; in strict philosophy it is sexless; but the female aspect is the first it assumes in human conceptions, its subsequent materialisation in any philosophy depending on the degree of the spirituality of the race or nation that produced the system. For instance: in the Kabbala of the Talmudists IT is called AIN-SOPH, the endless, the boundless, the infinite (the attribute being always negative), which *absolute* Principle is yet referred to as *He!!* From it, this negative, Boundless Circle of Infinite Light, emanates the first Sephira, the Crown, which the Talmudists call " Torah," the law, explaining that she is the wife of Ain-Soph. This is anthropomorphising the Spiritual with a vengeance.

Q. Is it the same in the Hindu Philosophies?

A. Exactly the opposite. For if we turn to the Hindu cosmogonies, we find that Parabrahm is not even mentioned therein, but only Mulaprakriti. The latter is, so to speak, the lining or aspect of Parabrahm in the invisible universe. Mulaprakriti means the Root of Nature or Matter. But Parabrahm cannot be called the " Root," for it is the absolute *Rootless Root* of all. Therefore, we must begin with Mulaprakriti, or the Veil of this unknowable. Here again we see that the first is the Mother Goddess, the reflection or the subjective root, on the first plane of Substance. Then follows, issuing from, or rather residing in, this Mother Goddess, the unmanifested Logos, he who is both her Son and Husband at once, called the " concealed Father." From these proceeds the first-manifested Logos, or Spirit, and the Son from whose substance emanate the Seven Logoi, whose synthesis, viewed as one collective Force, becomes the Architect of the Visible Universe. They are the Elohim of the Jews.

Q. What aspect of Space, or the unknown deity, called in the Vedas "THAT," *which is mentioned further on, is here called the " Eternal Parent"?*

A. It is the Vedantic Mulaprakriti, and the Svâbhâvat of the Buddhists, or that androgynous *something* of which we have been speaking, which is both differentiated and undifferentiated. In its first principle it is a pure abstraction, which becomes differentiated only when it is transformed, in the process of time, into Prakriti. If compared with the human principles it corresponds to Buddhi, while Atma would correspond to Parabrahm, Manas to Mahat, and so on.

Q. What, then, are the seven layers of Space, for in the "Proem" we read about the " Seven-Skinned Mother-Father"?

A. Plato and Hermes Trismegistus would have regarded this as the *Divine Thought*, and Aristotle would have viewed this " Mother-Father " as the " privation " of matter. It is that which will become the seven planes of being, commencing with the spiritual and passing through the psychic to the material plane. The seven planes of thought or the seven states of consciousness correspond to these planes. All these septenaries are symbolized by the seven " Skins."

Q. The divine ideas in the Divine Mind? But the Divine Mind is not yet.

A. The Divine Mind *is*, and must be, before differentiation takes place. It is called the divine Ideation, which is eternal in its Potentiality and periodical in its Potency, when it becomes *Mahat, Anima Mundi* or Universal Soul. But remember that, however you name it, each of these conceptions has its most metaphysical, most material, and also intermediate aspects.

Q. What is the meaning of the term " Ever invisible robes " ?

A. It is of course, as every allegory in the Eastern philosophies, a figurative expression. Perhaps it may be the hypothetical Protyle that Professor Crookes is in search of, but which can certainly never be found on this our earth or plane. It is the non-differentiated substance or spiritual matter.

Q. Is it what is called " Laya " ?

A. " Robes " and all are in the *Laya* condition, the point from which, or at which, the primordial substance begins to differentiate and thus gives birth to the universe and all in it.

Q. Are the " invisible robes " so called because they are not objective to any differentiation of consciousness.

A. Say rather, invisible to finite consciousness, if such consciousness were possible at that stage of evolution. Even for the Logos, Mulaprakriti is a veil, the Robes in which the Absolute is enveloped. Even the Logos cannot perceive the Absolute, say the Vedantins.*

Q. Is Mulaprakriti the correct term to use?

A. The Mulaprakriti of the Vedantins is the Aditi of the Vedas. The Vedanta philosophy means literally "the end or Synthesis of all knowledge." Now there are six schools of Hindu philosophy, which, however, will be found, on strict analysis, to agree perfectly in substance. Fundamentally they are identical, but there is such a wealth of names, such a quantity of side issues, details, and ornamentations—some emanations being their own fathers, and fathers born from their own daughters —that one becomes lost as in a jungle. State anything you please from the esoteric standpoint to a Hindu, and, if he so wishes, he can, from his own particular system, contradict or refute you. Each of the six schools has its own peculiar views and terms. So that unless the terminology of one school is adopted and used throughout the discussion, there is great danger of misunderstanding.

---

*Vide Mr. Subba Row's four Lectures, *Notes on the Bhagavat Gita*.

Q. Then the same identical term is used in quite a different sense by different philosophies? For instance, Buddhi has one meaning in the Esoteric and quite a different sense in the Sankya philosophy. Is not this so?

A. Precisely, and quite a different sense in the Vishnu Purana, which speaks of seven Prakritis emanating from Mahat, and calls the latter Maha-Buddhi. Fundamentally, however, the ideas are the same, though the terms differ with each school, and the correct sense is lost in this maze of personifications. It would, perhaps, if possible, be best to invent for ourselves a new nomenclature. Owing, however, to the poverty of European languages, especially English, in philosophical terms, the undertaking would be somewhat difficult.

Q. Could not the term "Protyle" be employed to represent the Laya condition?

A. Scarcely; the Protyle of Professor Crookes is probably used to denote homogeneous matter on the most material plane of all, whereas the *substance* symbolized by the "Robes" of the "Eternal Parent" is on the seventh plane of matter counting upwards, or rather from without within. This can never be discovered on the lowest, or rather most outward and material plane.

Q. Is there, then, on each of the seven planes, matter relatively homogeneous for every plane?

A. That is so; but such matter is homogeneous only for those who are on the same plane of perception; so that if the Protyle of modern science is ever discovered, it will be homogeneous only to us. The illusion may last for some time, perhaps until the sixth race, for humanity is ever changing, physically and mentally, and let us hope spiritually too, perfecting itself more and more with every race and sub-race.

Q. Would it not be a great mistake to use any term which has been used by scientists with another meaning? Protoplasm had once almost the same sense as Protyle, but its meaning has now become narrowed.

A. It would most decidedly; the *Hyle* (ὕλη) of the Greeks, however, most certainly did not apply to the matter of this plane, for they adopted it from the Chaldean cosmogony, where it was used in a highly metaphysical sense.

Q. But the word Hyle is now used by the materialists to express very nearly the same idea as that to which we apply the term Mulaprakriti.

A. It may be so; but Dr. Lewins and his brave half-dozen of

Hylo-Idealists are hardly of this opinion, for in their system the metaphysical meaning is entirely disregarded and lost sight of.

Q. Then perhaps after all Laya is the best term to use?

A. Not so, for Laya does not mean any particular something or some plane or other, but denotes a state or condition. It is a Sanskrit term, conveying the idea of something in an undifferentiated and changeless state, a zero point wherein all differentiation ceases.

Q. The first differentiation would represent matter on its seventh plane: must we not, therefore, suppose that Professor Crookes' Protyle is also matter on its seventh plane?

A. The ideal Protyle of Professor Crookes is matter in that state which he calls the " zero-point."

Q. That is to say, the Laya point of this plane?

A. It is not at all clear whether Professor Crookes is occupied with other planes or admits their existence. The object of his search is the protylic atom, which, as no one has ever seen it, is simply a new working hypothesis of Science. For what in reality is an atom?

Q. It is a convenient definition of what is supposed to be, or rather a convenient term to divide up, a molecule.

A. But surely they must have come by this time to the conclusion that the atom is no more a convenient term than the supposed seventy odd elements. It has been the custom to laugh at the four and five elements of the ancients; but now Professor Crookes has come to the conclusion that, strictly speaking, there is no such thing as a chemical element at all. In fact, so far from discovering the atom, a single simple molecule has not yet been arrived at.

Q. It should be remembered that Dalton, who first spoke on the subject, called it the " Atomic Theory."

A. Quite so; but, as shown by Sir W. Hamilton, the term is used in an erroneous sense by the modern schools of science, which, while laughing at metaphysics, apply a purely metaphysical term to physics, so that nowadays "theory" begins to usurp the prerogatives of "axiom."

Q. What are the " Seven Eternities," and how can there be such a division in Pralaya, when there is no one to be conscious of time?

A. The modern astronomer knows the "ordinances of Heaven" by no means better than his ancient brother did. If asked whether he could "bring forth Mazzaroth in his season," or if he was with "him" who

" spread out the sky," he would have to answer sadly, just as Job did, in the negative. Yet this in no wise prevents him from speculating about the age of the Sun, Moon, and Earth, and "calculating" geological periods from that time when there was not a living man, with or without consciousness, on earth. Why, therefore, should not the same privilege be granted to the ancients?

Q. But why should the term " Seven Eternities" be employed?

A. The term "Seven Eternities" is employed owing to the invariable law of analogy. As Manvantara is divided into seven periods, so is Pralaya; as day is composed of twelve hours so is night. Can we say that because we are asleep during the night and lose consciousness of time, that therefore the hours do not strike? Pralaya is the "Night" after the Manvantaric "Day." There is no one by, and consciousness is asleep with the rest. But since it exists, and is in full activity during Manvantara; and since we are fully alive to the fact that the law of analogy and periodicity is immutable, and, being so, that it must act equally at both ends, why cannot the phrase be used?

Q. But how can an eternity be counted?

A. Perhaps the query arises owing to the general misunderstanding of the term "Eternity." We Westerns are foolish enough to speculate about that which has neither beginning nor end, and we imagine that the ancients must have done the same. They did not, however: no philosopher in days of old ever took "Eternity" to mean beginningless and endless duration. Neither the Æons of the Greeks nor the Naroses convey this meaning. In fact, they had no word to convey this precise sense. Parabrahm, Ain-Soph, and the *Zeruana-Akerne* of the Avesta alone represent such an Eternity; all the other periods are finite and astronomical, based on tropical years and other enormous cycles. The word Æon, which in the Bible is translated by Eternity, means not only a finite period, but also an angel and being.

Q. But is it not correct to say that in Pralaya too there is the " Great Breath"?

A. Assuredly: for the "Great Breath" is ceaseless, and is, so to speak, the universal and eternal *perpetuum mobile?*

Q. If so, it is impossible to divide it into periods, for this does away with the idea of absolute and complete nothingness. It seems somewhat incompatible that any " number" of periods should be spoken of, although one might speak of so many outbreathings and indrawings of the " Great Breath."

A. This would make away with the idea of absolute Rest, were not this absoluteness of Rest counteracted by the absoluteness of Motion. Therefore one expression is as good as the other. There is a magnificent poem on Pralaya, written by a very ancient Rishi, who compares the motion of the Great Breath during Pralaya to the rhythmical motions of the Unconscious Ocean.

Q. The difficulty is when the word "eternity" is used instead of "Æon."

A. Why should a Greek word be used when there is a more familiar expression, especially as it is fully explained in the *Secret Doctrine?* You may call it a *relative*, or a Manvantaric and Pralayic eternity, if you like.

Q. Is the relation of Pralaya and Manvantara strictly analogous to the relations between sleeping and waking?

A. In a certain sense only; during night we all exist personally, and *are* individually, though we sleep and may be unconscious of so living. But during Pralaya every thing differentiated, as every unit, disappears from the phenomenal universe and is merged in, or rather transferred into, the One noumenal. Therefore, *de facto*, there is a great difference.

Q. Sleep has been called the "Shady side of life;" may Pralaya be called the shady side of Cosmic life?

A. It may in a certain way be called so. Pralaya is dissolution of the visible into the invisible, the heterogeneous into the homogeneous—a time of rest, therefore. Even cosmic matter, indestructible though it be in its essence, must have a time of rest, and return to its *Layam* state. The absoluteness of the all-containing One essence has to manifest itself equally in rest and activity.

Sloka (2). TIME WAS NOT, FOR IT LAY ASLEEP IN THE INFINITE BOSOM OF DURATION.

Q. What is the difference between Time and Duration?

A. Duration *is;* it has neither beginning nor end. How can you call that which has neither beginning nor end, Time? Duration is beginningless and endless; Time is finite.

Q. Is, then, Duration the infinite, and Time the finite conception?

A. Time can be divided; Duration—in our philosophy, at least—cannot. Time is divisible in Duration—or, as you put it, the one is something *within* Time and Space, whereas the other is outside of both.

Q. The only way one can define Time is by the motion of the earth

A. But we can also define Time in our conceptions.

Q. Duration, rather?

A. No, Time; for as to Duration, it is impossible to divide it or set up landmarks therein. Duration with us is the one eternity, not relative, but absolute.

Q. Can it be said that the essential idea of Duration is existence?

A. No; existence has limited and definite periods, whereas Duration, having neither beginning nor end, is a perfect abstraction which contains Time. Duration is like Space, which is an abstraction too, and is equally without beginning or end. It is in its concretency and limitation only that it becomes a representation and something. Of course the distance between two points is called space; it may be enormous or it may be infinitesimal, yet it will always be space. But all such specifications are divisions in human conception. In reality Space is what the ancients called the One invisible and unknown (now unknowable) Deity.

Q. Then Time is the same as Space, being one in the abstract?

A. As two abstractions they may be one; but this would apply to Duration and Abstract Space rather than to Time and Space.

Q. Space is the objective and Time the subjective side of all manifestation. In reality they are the only attributes of the infinite; but attribute is perhaps a bad term to use, inasmuch as they are, so to speak, co-extensive with the infinite. It may, however, be objected that they are nothing but the creations of our own intellect; simply the forms in which we cannot help conceiving things.

A. That sounds like an argument of our friends the Hylo-idealists; but here we speak of the noumenal and not of the phenomenal universe. In the occult catechism (*Vide Secret Doctrine*) it is asked: "What is that which always IS, which you cannot imagine as not *being*, do what you may?" The answer is—SPACE. For there may not be a single man in the universe to think of it, not a single eye to perceive it, nor a single brain to sense it, but still Space *is, ever was, and ever will be*, and you cannot make away with it.

Q. Because we cannot help thinking of it, perhaps?

A. Our thinking of it has nothing to do with the question. Try, rather, if you can think of anything with Space excluded and you will soon find out the impossibility of such a conception. Space exists where there is nothing else, and must so exist whether the Universe is one absolute vacuum or a full Pleroma.

Q. Modern Philosophers have reduced it to this, that space and time are nothing but attributes, nothing but accidents.

A. And they would be right, were their reduction the fruit of true science instead of being the result of *Avidya* and *Maya*. We find also Buddha saying that even Nirvâna, after all, is but *Maya*, or an illusion; but the Lord Buddha based what he said on *knowledge*, not *speculation*.

Q. But are eternal Space and Duration the only attributes of the Infinite?

A. Space and Duration, being eternal, cannot be called attributes, as they are only the *aspects* of that Infinite. Nor can that Infinite, if you mean by it The Absolute Principle, have any attributes whatever, as only that which is itself finite and conditioned can have any relation to something else. All this is philosophically wrong.

Q. We can conceive of no matter which is not extended, no extension which is not extension of something. Is it the same on higher planes? And if so, what is the substance which fills absolute space, and is it identical with that space?

A. If your "trained intellect" cannot conceive of any other kind of matter, perhaps one less trained but more open to spiritual perceptions can. It does not follow, because you say so, that such a conception of Space is the only one possible, even on our Earth. For even on this plane of ours there are other and various intellects, besides those of man, in creatures visible and invisible, from minds of subjective high and low Beings to objective animals and the lowest organisms, in short, "from the Deva to the elephant, from the elemental to the ant." Now, in relation to its own plane of conception and perception, the ant has as good an intellect as we have ourselves, and a better one; for though it cannot express it in words, yet, over and above instinct, the ant shows very high reasoning powers, as all of us know. Thus, finding on our own plane— if we credit the teachings of Occultism—so many and such varied states of consciousness and intelligence, we have no right to take into consideration and account only our own human consciousness, as though no other existed outside of it. And if we cannot presume to decide how far insect consciousness goes, how can we limit consciousness, of which Science knows nothing, to this plane.

Q. But why not? Surely natural science can discover all that has to be discovered, even in the ant?

A. Such is your view; to the occultist, however, such confidence is misplaced, in spite of Sir John Lubbock's labours. Science may speculate, but, with its present methods, will never be able to prove the certitude of such speculations. If a scientist could become an ant for a while, and think as an ant, and remember his experience on returning to his own sphere of consciousness, then only would he know something for certain of this interesting insect. As it is, he can only speculate, making inferences from the ant's behaviour.

Q. *The ant's conception of time and space are not our own, then. Is it this that you mean?*

A. Precisely; the ant has conceptions of time and space which are its own, not ours; conceptions which are entirely on another plane; we have, therefore, no right to deny *à priori* the existence of other planes only because we can form no idea of them, but which exist nevertheless—planes higher and lower than our own by many degrees, as witness the ant.

Q. *The difference between the animal and man from this point of view seems to be that the former is born more or less with all its faculties, and, generally speaking, does not appreciably gain on this, while the latter is gradually learning and improving. Is not that really the point?*

A. Just so; but you have to remember why: not because man has one "principle" more than the tiniest insect, but because man is a perfected animal, the vehicle of a fully developed *monad*, self-conscious and deliberately following its own line of progress, whereas in the insect, and even the higher animal, the higher triad of principles is absolutely dormant.

Q. *Is there any consciousness, or conscious being, to cognize and make a division of time at the first flutter of manifestation? In his Lecture on the Bhagavat Gita, Mr. Subba Row, in speaking of the First Logos, seems to imply both consciousness and intelligence.*

A. But he did not explain which Logos was referred to, and I believe he spoke in general. In the Esoteric Philosophy the First is the unmanifested, and the Second the manifested Logos. Iswara stands for that Second, and Nârâyana for the unmanifested Logos. Subba Row is an Adwaitee and a learned Vedantin, and explained from his standpoint. We do so from ours. In the *Secret Doctrine*, that from which the manifested Logos is born is translated by the "Eternal Mother-Father"; while in the Vishnu Purâna it is described as the Egg of the World, surrounded by seven skins, layers or zones. It is in this Golden Egg that Brahmâ, the male, is born and that Brahmâ is in reality the Second Logos or even the Third, according to the enumeration adopted; for a certainty he is not the First or highest, the point which is everywhere and nowhere. Mahat, in the Esoteric interpretations, is in reality the Third Logos or the Synthesis of the Seven creative rays, the Seven Logoi. Out of the seven so-called *Creations*, Mahat is the third, for it is the Universal and Intelligent Soul, Divine Ideation, combining the ideal plans and prototypes of all things in the manifested objective as well as subjective world. In the Sankhya and Purânic doctrines Mahat is the first product of *Pradhâna*, informed by Kshetrajna "Spirit-Substance." In Esoteric philosophy Kshetrajna is the name given to our informing Egos.

Q. Is it then the first manifestation in our objective universe?

A. It is the first Principle in it, made sensible or perceptible to divine though not human senses. But if we proceed from the Unknowable, we will find it to be the third, and corresponding to Manas, or rather Buddhi-Manas.

Q. Then the First Logos is the first point within the circle?

A. The point within the circle which has neither limit nor boundaries, nor can it have any name or attribute. This first unmanifested Logos is simultaneous with the line drawn across the diameter of the Circle. The first line or diameter is the Mother-Father; from it proceeds the Second Logos, which contains in itself the Third Manifested Word. In the Purânas, for instance, it is again said that the first production of Akâsa is Sound, and Sound means in this case the "Word," the expression of the unuttered thought, the manifested Logos, that of the Greeks and Platonists and St. John. Dr. Wilson and other Orientalists speak of this conception of the Hindus as an absurdity, for according to them Akâsa and Chaos are identical. But if they knew that Akâsa and Pradhâna are but two aspects of the same thing, and remember that Mahat, the *divine ideation on our plane*—is that manifested *Sound* or Logos, they would laugh at themselves and their own ignorance.

Q. With reference to the following passage, what is the consciousness which takes cognizance of time? Is the consciousness of time limited to the plane of waking physical consciousness, or does it exist on higher planes? In the Secret Doctrine, I., 37, it is said that:—"*Time is only an illusion produced by the succession of states of consciousness as we travel through eternal duration, and it does not exist where no consciousness exists.*"

A. Here consciousness only on our plane is meant, not the eternal *divine* Consciousness which we call the Absolute. The consciousness of time, in the present sense of the word, does not exist even in sleep ; much less, therefore, can it exist in the essentially absolute. Can the sea be said to have a conception of time in its rhythmical striking on the shore, or in the movement of its waves? The Absolute cannot be said to have a consciousness, or, at any rate, a consciousness such as we have here. It has neither consciousness, nor desire, nor wish, nor thought, because it is absolute thought, absolute desire, absolute consciousness, absolute " all."

Q. Is it what we refer to as BE-NESS, *or* SAT ?

A. Our kind critics have found the word "Be-ness" very amusing, but there is no other way of translating the Sanskrit term, *Sat*. It is not existence, for existence can only apply to *phenomena*, never to *noumena*, the very etymology of the Latin term contradicting such assertion, as *ex* means "from" or "out of," and *sistere* "to stand" ; therefore, something appearing being then where it was not before. Existence, moreover, implies something having a beginning and an end. How can the term, therefore, be applied to that which ever was, and of which it cannot be predicated that it ever issued from something else ?

Q. The Hebrew Jehovah was " I am."

A. And so was Ormuzd, the Ahura-Mazda of the old Mazdeans. In this sense every man as much as every God can boast of his existence, saying " I am that I am."

Q. But surely " Be-ness" has some connection with the word " to be"?

A. Yes ; but "Be-ness" is not *being*, for it is equally *non-being*. We cannot conceive it, for our intellects are finite and our language far more limited and conditioned even than our minds. How, therefore, can we express that which we can only conceive of by a series of negatives ?

Q. A German could more easily express it by the word "sein"; "das sein" would be a very good equivalent of "Be-ness"; the latter term may sound absurd to unaccustomed English ears, but "das sein" is a perfectly familiar term and idea to a German. But we were speaking of consciousness in Space and Time.

A. This Consciousness is finite, having beginning and end. But where is the word for such finite Consciousness which still, owing to *Mâya*, believes itself infinite ? Not even the Devachanee is conscious of time. All is present in Devachan ; there is no past, otherwise the

Ego would recall and regret it; no future, or it would desire to have it. Seeing, therefore, that Devachan is a state of bliss in which everything is present, the Devachanee is said to have no conception or idea of time; everything is to him as in a vivid dream, a reality.

Q. But we may dream a lifetime in half a second, being conscious of a succession of states of consciousness, events taking place one after the other.

A. After the dream only; no such consciousness exists while dreaming.

Q. May we not compare the recollection of a dream to a person giving the description of a picture, and having to mention all the parts and details because he cannot present the whole before the mind's eye of the listener?

A. That is a very good analogy.

II.

Meeting held at 17, Lansdowne Road, London, W., on January 17th, 1889, Mr. T. B. HARBOTTLE in the Chair.

STANZA I. (*continued*).

Sloka (3). . . . . . UNIVERSAL MIND WAS NOT, FOR THERE WERE NO AH-HI (*celestial beings*) TO CONTAIN (*hence manifest*) IT.

Q. This sloka seems to imply that the Universal Mind has no existence apart from the Ah-hi; but in the Commentary it is stated that:

"During Pralaya the Universal Mind remains as a permanent possibility of mental action, or as that abstract absolute thought of which mind is the concrete relative manifestation, and that the Ah-hi are the vehicle for divine universal thought and will. They are the intelligent forces which give to nature her laws, while they themselves act according to laws imposed upon them by still higher powers, and are the hierarchy of spiritual beings through which the universal mind comes into action."*

The Commentary suggests that the Ah-hi are not themselves the Universal Mind, but only the vehicle for its manifestation.

A. The meaning of this sloka is, I think, very clear; it means that, as there are no finite differentiated minds during Pralaya, it is just as though there were no mind at all, because there is nothing *to contain or perceive it*. There is nothing to receive and reflect the ideation of the Absolute Mind; therefore, *it is not*. Everything outside of the Absolute and immutable Sat (Be-ness), is necessarily finite and conditioned, since it has beginning and end. Therefore, since the "Ah-hi were not," there was no Universal Mind as a manifestation. A distinction had to be made between the Absolute Mind, which is ever present, and its reflection and manifestation in the Ah-hi, who, being on the highest plane, reflect the universal mind collectively at the first flutter of Manvantara. After which they begin the work of evolution of all the lower forces throughout the seven planes, down to the lowest—our own. The Ah-hi are the primordial seven rays, or *Logoi*, emanated from the first Logos, *triple*, yet one in its essence.

---

* S. D., I. 38.

Q. Then the Ah-hi and Universal Mind are necessary complements of one another?

A. Not at all: Universal or Absolute Mind always *is* during Pralaya as well as Manvantara; it is immutable. The Ah-hi are the highest Dhyanis, the Logoi as just said, those who begin the downward evolution, or emanation. During Pralaya there are no Ah-hi, because they come into being only with the first *radiation* of the Universal Mind, which, *per se,* cannot be differentiated, and the radiation from which is the first *dawn* of Manvantara. The Absolute is dormant, latent mind, and cannot be otherwise in true metaphysical perception; it is only Its shadow which becomes differentiated in the collectivity of these Dhyanis.

Q. Does this mean that it was absolute consciousness, but is so no longer?

A. It is *absolute consciousness* eternally, which consciousness becomes *relative consciousness* periodically, at every " Manvantaric dawn." Let us picture to ourselves this latent or potential consciousness as a kind of vacuum in a vessel. Break the vessel, and what becomes of the vacuum; where shall we look for it? It has disappeared; it is everywhere and nowhere. It is something, yet *nothing:* a *vacuum,* yet a *plenum.* But what in reality is a vacuum as understood by Modern Science—a homogeneous something, or what? Is not absolute Vacuum a figment of our fancy? A pure negation, a supposed Space where nothing exists? This being so, destroy the vessel, and—to our perceptions at any rate—nothing exists. Therefore, the Stanza puts it very correctly; "Universal Mind was not," because there was no vehicle to contain it.

Q. What are the higher powers which condition the Ah-hi?

A. They cannot be called powers; *power* or perhaps Potentiality would be better. The Ah-hi are conditioned by the awakening into manifestation of the periodical, universal LAW, which becomes successively active and inactive. It is by this law that they are conditioned or formed, not created. "Created" is an impossible term to use in Philosophy.

Q. Then the power or Potentiality which precedes and is higher than the Ah-hi, is the law which necessitates manifestation.

A. Just so; periodical manifestation. When the hour strikes, the law comes into action, and the Ah-hi appear on the first rung of the ladder of manifestation.

Q. But surely this is THE *law and not* A *law?*

A. Precisely, since it is absolute and " Secondless "—therefore it is not an attribute, but that Absoluteness itself.

Q. The great difficulty is to account for this law?

A. That would be trying to go beyond the first manifestation and supreme causality. It will take all our limited intellect to vaguely understand even the latter; try as we may, we can never, limited as we are, approach the Absolute, which is to us, at our present stage of mental development, merely a logical speculation, though dating back to thousands and thousands of years.

Q. With reference to the sloka under discussion, would not " cosmic mind" be a better term than "universal mind"?

A. No; cosmic mind appears at the third stage, or degree, and is confined or limited to the manifested universe. In the Purânas Mahat (the "great" Principle of mind, or Intellect) appears only at the third of the Seven "Creations" or stages of evolution. Cosmic Mind is Mahat, or divine ideation in active (creative) operation, and thus only the periodical manifestation *in time* and *in actu* of the Eternal Universal Mind— *in potentia*. In strict truth, Universal Mind, being only another name for the Absolute, *out of time and Space*, this Cosmic Ideation, or Mind, is not an evolution at all (least of all a "creation"), but simply one of the aspects of the former, which knows no change, which ever was, which is, and will be. Thus, I say again, the sloka implies that universal ideation was not, *i.e.*, did not exist for perception, because there were no minds to perceive it, since Cosmic Mind was still latent, or a mere potentiality. As the stanzas speak of manifestation, we are compelled so to translate them, and not from any other standpoint.

Q. We use the word "cosmic" as applied to the manifested universe in all its forms. The sloka apparently does not refer to this, but to the first absolute Consciousness, or Non-consciousness, and seems to imply that the absolute consciousness could not be that universal mind because it was not, or could not be, expressed: there was, therefore, no expression for it. But it may be objected that though there was no expression for it, still it was there. Can we say that, like Sat, it was and was not?

A. That will not help the interpretation.

Q. When it is said that it was not, the idea conveyed then is that it was not in the Absolute?

A. By no means; simply "it was not."

Q. There seems to be a distinction, certainly; for if we could say " it was," it would be taking a very one-sided view of the idea of Sat, and equivalent to saying that Sat was BEING. *Still, someone may say that the phrase " Universal Mind was not," as it stands, suggests that it is a manifestation, but mind is not a manifestation.*

A. Mind, in the act of ideation, is a manifestation; but Universal Mind is not the same thing, as no conditioned and relative act can be predicted of that which is Absolute. Universal ideation was as soon as the Ah-hi appeared, and continues throughout the Manvantara.

Q. To what cosmic plane do the Ah-hi, here spoken of, belong?

A. They belong to the first, second, and third planes—the last plane being really the starting point of the primordial manifestation—the objective reflection of the unmanifested. Like the Pythagorean *Monas*, the first Logos, having emanated the first triad, disappears into silence and darkness.

Q. Does this mean that the three Logoi emanated from the primordial Radiation in Macrocosm correspond to Atma, Buddhi, and Manas, in the Microcosm?

A. Just so; they correspond, but must not be confounded with them. We are now speaking of the Macrocosm at the first flutter of Manvantaric dawn, when evolution begins, and not of Microcosm or Man.

Q. Are the three planes to which the three Logoi belong simultaneous emanations, or do they evolve one from another?

A. It is most misleading to apply mechanical laws to the higher metaphysics of cosmogony, or to space and time, as we know them for neither existed then. The reflection of the triad in space and time or the objective universe comes later.

Q. Have the Ah-hi been men in previous Manvantaras, or will they become so?

A. Every living creature, of whatever description, was, is, or will become a human being in one or another Manvantara.

Q. But do they in this Manvantara remain permanently on the same very exalted plane during the whole period of the life-cycle?

A. If you mean by "life cycle" a duration of time which extends over fifteen figures, then my answer is most decidedly—no. The "Ah-hi" pass through all the planes, beginning to manifest on the third. Like all other Hierarchies, on the highest plane they are *arupa*, *i.e.*, formless, bodiless, without any substance, mere breaths. On the second plane, they first approach to Rupa, or form. On the third, they became Manasa-putras, those who became incarnated in men. With every plane they reach they are called by different names—there is a continual differentiation of their original homogeneous substance; we call it substance, although in reality it is no substance of which we can conceive. Later, they become Rupa—ethereal forms.

Q. Then the Ah-hi of this Manvantara . . . ?

A. Exist no longer; they have long ago become Planetary, Solar, Lunar, and lastly, incarnating Egos, for, as said, "they are the collective hosts of spiritual beings."

Q. But it was stated above that the Ah-hi did not become men in this Manvantara.

A. Nor do they as the formless "Ah-hi." But they do as their own transformations. The Manvantaras should not be confounded. The fifteen-figure Manvantaric cycle applies to the solar system; but there is a Manvantara which relates to the whole of the objective universe, the Mother-Father, and many minor Manvantaras. The slokas relating to the former have been generally selected, and only two or three relating to the latter given. Many slokas, therefore, have been omitted because of their difficult nature.

Q. Then, on reawakening, will the men of one Manvantara have to pass through a stage corresponding to the Ah-hi stage in the next Manvantara?

A. In some of the Manvantaras, the tail is in the mouth of the serpent. Think over this Symbolism.

Q. A man can choose what he will think about; can the analogy be applied to the Ah-hi?

A. No; because a man has free will and the Ah-hi have none. They are obliged to act simultaneously, for the law under which they must act gives them the impulse. Free will can only exist in a Man who has both mind and consciousness, which act and make him perceive things both within and without himself. The "Ah-hi" are Forces, not human Beings.

Q. But are they not conscious agents in the work?

A. Conscious in as far as they act within the universal consciousness. But the consciousness of the Manasa-putra on the third plane is quite different. It is only then that they become *Thinkers*. Besides, Occultism, unlike modern Science, maintains that every atom of matter, when once differentiated, becomes endowed with *its own* kind of Consciousness. Every *cell* in the human body (as in every animal) is endowed with its own peculiar discrimination, instinct, and, speaking relatively, with intelligence.

Q. Can the Ah-hi be said to be enjoying bliss?

A. How can they be subject to bliss or non-bliss? Bliss can only be appreciated, and becomes such when suffering is known.

Q. But there is a distinction between happiness and bliss.

A. Granting that there may be, still there can be neither happiness nor bliss without a contrasting experience of suffering and pain.

Q. But we understand that bliss, as the state of the Absolute, was intended to be referred to.

A. This is still more illogical. How can the ABSOLUTE be said to *feel?* The Absolute can have no condition nor attribute. It is only that which is finite and differentiated which can have any feeling or attitude predicated of it.

Q. Then the Ah-hi cannot be said to be conscious intelligences, when intelligence is so complex?

A. Perhaps the term is erroneous, but owing to the poverty of European languages there seems to be no other choice.

Q. But perhaps a phrase would represent the idea more correctly? The term seems to mean a force which is a unity, not a complex action and reaction of several forces, which would be implied by the word "intelligence." The noumenal aspect of phenomenal force would perhaps better express the idea.

A. Or perhaps we may represent to ourselves the idea as a flame, a unity; the rays from this flame will be complex, each acting in its own straight line.

Q. But they only become complex when they find receptacles in lower forms.

A. Just so; still the Ah-hi are the flame from which the rays stream forth, becoming more and more differentiated as they fall deeper into matter, until they finally reach this world of ours, with its teeming millions of inhabitants and sensuous beings, and then they become truly complex.

Q. The Ah-hi, then, considered as a primary essence, would be unity? Can we regard them as such?

A. You may; but the strict truth is that they only proceed from unity, and are the first of its seven rays.

Q. Then can we call them the reflection of unity?

A. Are not the prismatic rays fundamentally one single white ray? From the one they become three; from the three, seven; from which seven primaries they fall into infinitude. Referring back to the so-called "consciousness" of the Ah-hi, that consciousness cannot be judged by the standard of human perceptions. It is on quite another plane.

Q. " During deep sleep, mind is not on the material plane"; is it therefore to be inferred that during this period mind is active on another plane? Is there any definition of the characteristics which distinguish mind in the waking state from mind during the sleep of the body?

A. There is, of course; but I do not think that a discussion upon it would be pertinent or useful now; suffice to say that often the reasoning faculty of the higher mind may be asleep, and the instinctual mind be fully awake. It is the physiological distinction between the cerebrum and the cerebellum; the one sleeps and the other is awake.

Q. What is meant by the term instinctual mind?

A. The instinctual mind finds expression through the cerebellum, and is also that of the animals. With man during sleep the functions of the cerebrum cease, and the cerebellum carries him on to the Astral plane, a still more unreal state than even the waking plane of illusion; for so we call this state which the majority of you think so real. And the Astral plane is still more deceptive, because it reflects indiscriminately the good and the bad, and is so chaotic.

Q. The fundamental conditions of the mind in the waking state are space and time: do these exist for the mind (Manas) during the sleep of the physical body?

A. Not as we know them. Moreover, the answer depends on which *Manas* you mean—the higher or the lower. It is only the latter which is susceptible of hallucinations about space and time; for instance, a man in the dreaming state may live in a few seconds the events of a lifetime.* For the perceptions and apprehensions of the Higher Ego there is neither space nor time.

---

* See the discussion on dreams appended to the first No. of the TRANSACTIONS.

Q. Manas is said to be the vehicle of Buddhi, but the universal mind has been spoken of as a Maha-Buddhi. What then is the distinction between the terms Manas and Buddhi, employed in a universal sense, and Manas and Buddhi as manifested in man?

A. Cosmic Buddhi, the emanation of the Spiritual Soul *Alaya*, is the vehicle of Mahat only when that Buddhi corresponds to Prakriti. Then it is called Maha-Buddhi. This Buddhi differentiates through seven planes, whereas the Buddhi in man is the vehicle of Atman, which vehicle is of the essence of the highest plane of Akasa and therefore does not differentiate. The difference between Manas and Buddhi in man is the same as the difference between the Manasa-Putra and the Ah-hi in Kosmos.

Q. Manas is mind, and the Ah-hi, it is said, can no more have any individual Mind, or that which we call mind, on this plane than Buddhi can. Can there be Consciousness without Mind?

A. Not on this plane of matter. But why not on some other and higher plane? Once we postulate a Universal Mind, both the brain, the mind's vehicle, and Consciousness, its faculty, must be quite different on a higher plane from what they are here. They are nearer to the *Absolute* ALL, and must therefore be represented by a substance infinitely more homogeneous; something *sui generis*, and entirely beyond the reach of our intellectual perceptions. Let us call or imagine it an incipient and incognizable state of primeval differentiation. On that higher plane, as it seems to me, Mahat—the great *Manvantaric* Principle of Intelligence—acts as a Brain, through which the Universal and Eternal Mind radiates the Ah-hi, representing the resultant Consciousness or ideation. As the shadow of this primordial *triangle* falls lower and lower through the descending planes, it becomes with every stage more material.

Q. It becomes the plane on which Consciousness perceives objective manifestations. Is it so?

A. Yes. But here we come face to face with the great problem of Consciousness, and shall have to fight Materialism. For what is Consciousness? According to modern Science it is a faculty of the Mind like volition. We say so too; but add that while Consciousness is not a thing *per se*, Mind is distinctly—in its Manvantaric functions at least—an Entity. Such is the opinion of all the Eastern Idealists.

Q. It is, however, the fashion nowadays to speak slightingly of the idea that the mind is an entity.

A. Nevertheless, mind is a term perfectly synonymous with Soul. Those who deny the existence of the latter will of course contend that there is no such thing as consciousness apart from brain, and at death consciousness ceases. Occultists, on the contrary, affirm that consciousness exists after death, and that then only the real consciousness and freedom of the Ego commences, when it is no longer impeded by terrestrial matter.

Q. Perhaps the former view arises from limiting the meaning of the term " consciousness" to the faculty of perception?

A. If so, occultism is entirely opposed to such a view.

Sloka (4). THE SEVEN WAYS TO BLISS *(Moksha or Nirvana)* WERE NOT.* THE GREAT CAUSES OF MISERY *(Nidâna and Maya)* WERE NOT, FOR THERE WAS NO ONE TO PRODUCE AND GET ENSNARED BY THEM.

Q. What are the seven ways to bliss?

A. They are certain faculties of which the student will know more when he goes deeper into occultism.

Q. Are the Four Truths of the Hinayâna School the same as those mentioned by Sir Edwin Arnold in " The Light of Asia "; the first of which is the Path of Sorrow; the second of Sorrow's cause: the third of Sorrow's ceasing; and the fourth is the WAY?

A. All this is theological and exoteric, and to be found in all the Buddhist scriptures; and the above seems to be taken from Singhalese or Southern Buddhism. The subject, however, is far more fully treated of in the Aryasanga School. Still even there the four truths have one meaning for the regular priest of the Yellow Robe, and quite another for the real Mystics.

Q. Are Nidâna and Maya (the great causes of misery) aspects of the Absolute?

A. Nidâna means the concatenation of cause and effect; the twelve Nidânas are the enumeration of the chief causes which produce the severest reaction or effects under the Karmic law. Although there is no connection between the terms Nidâna and Maya in themselves, Maya being simply illusion, yet if we consider the universe as Maya or

---

*Vide *The Voice of the Silence*; Fragment III., *The Seven Portals*.

illusion, then certainly the Nidânas, as being moral agents in the universe, are included in Maya. It is Maya, illusion or ignorance, which awakens Nidânas; and the cause or causes having been produced, the effects follow according to Karmic law. To take an instance: we all regard ourselves as Units, although essentially we are one indivisible Unit, drops in the ocean of Being, not to be distinguished from other drops. Having then produced this cause, the whole discord of life follows immediately as an effect; in reality it is the endeavour of nature to restore harmony and maintain equilibrium. It is this sense of separateness which is the root of all evil.

Q. Perhaps it would therefore be better to separate the two terms, and state whether Maya in an aspect of the Absolute?

A. This can hardly be so, since Maya is the Cause, and at the same time an aspect, of differentiation, if of anything. Moreover, the Absolute can never be differentiated. Maya is a manifestation; the Absolute can have no manifestation, but only a reflection, a shadow which is radiated periodically from it—not *by* it.

Q. Yet Maya is said to be the Cause of manifestation or differentiation?

A. What of that? Certainly if there were no Maya there would be no differentiation, or, rather, no objective universe would be perceived. But this does not make of it an aspect of the Absolute, but simply something coeval and coexistent with the manifested Universe or the heterogeneous differentiation of pure Homogeneity.

Q. By a parity of reason, then, if no differentiation, no Maya? But we are speaking of Maya now as THE CAUSE *of the Universe, so that the moment we get behind differentiation, we may ask ourselves—Where is Maya?*

A. Maya is everywhere, and in every *thing* that has a beginning and an end; therefore, every *thing* is an *aspect* of that which is eternal, and in that sense, of course Maya itself is an aspect of SAT, or that which *is* eternally present in the universe, whether during Manvantara or Mahapralaya. Only remember that it has been said of even Nirvâna that it is only Maya when compared with the Absolute.

Q. Is then Maya a collective term for all manifestations?

A. I do not think this would explain the term. Maya is the perceptive faculty of every Ego which considers itself a Unit separate from, and independent of, the One infinite and eternal SAT, or "be-ness."

Maya is explained in *exoteric* philosophy and the Purânas, as the personified active Will *of the Creative God*—the latter being but a personified *Maya* himself—a passing deception of the senses of man, who began anthropomorphizing pure abstraction from the beginning of his speculations. Maya, in the conception of an orthodox Hindu, is quite different from the Maya of a Vedantin Idealist or an Occultist. The Vedanta states that Maya, or the deceptive influence of illusion alone, constitutes belief in the *real* existence of matter or anything differentiated. The Bhagavata Purâna identifies Maya with Prakriti (manifested nature and matter). Do not some advanced European metaphysicians, such as Kant, Schopenhauer, and others, assert the same? Of course they got their ideas about it from the East—especially from Buddhism; yet the doctrine of the unreality of this universe has been pretty correctly worked out by our philosophers—on general lines, at any rate. Now, although no two people can see things and objects in exactly the same way, and that each of us sees them in his own way, yet all labour more or less under illusions, and chiefly under the great illusion (Maya) that they are, as personalities, distinct beings from other beings, and that even their *Selves* or Egos will prevail in the eternity (or sempiternity, at any rate) as such; whereas not only we ourselves, but the whole visible and invisible universe, are only a temporary part of the one beginningless and endless WHOLE, or that which ever was, is, and will be.

Q. The term seems to apply to the complex points of differentiation: differentiation applying to the unit and Maya to the collection of units. But we may now put a side question.

With regard to the preceding part of the discussion, reference has been made to the cerebrum and cerebellum, and the latter described as the instinctual organ. An animal is supposed to have an instinctive mind; but the cerebellum is said to be simply the organ of vegetative life, and to control the functions of the body alone; whereas the sensual mind is the mind into which the senses open, and there can be no thought or ideation, nothing of which we predicate intellect or instinct anywhere, except in that part of the brain assigned to such functions, namely, the cerebrum.

A. However that may be, this cerebellum is the organ of instinctual animal functions, which reflect themselves in, or produce, dreams which for the most part are chaotic and inconsequent. Dreams, however, which are remembered, and present a sequence of events, are due to the vision of the higher Ego.

Q. Is not the cerebellum what we may call the organ of habit?

A. Being instinctual, it may very well be called so, I believe.

Q. Except that habit may be referred to what we may call the present stage of existence, and instinct to a past stage.

A. Whatever the name may be, the cerebellum alone—as you were already told (*vide* " On Dreams," *Appendix*)—functions during sleeep, not the cerebrum ; and the dreams, or emanations, or instinctive feelings, which we experience on waking, are the result of such activity.

Q. The consecutiveness is brought about entirely by the co-ordinating faculty. But surely the cerebrum also acts, a proof of which is that the nearer we approach the sleep-waking state the more vivid our dreams become.

A. Quite so, *when* you are waking ; but not before. We may compare this state of the cerebellum to a bar of metal, or something of the same nature, which has been heated during the day and emanates or radiates heat during the night ; so the energy of the brain radiates unconsciously during the night.

Q. Still we cannot say that the brain is incapable of registering impressions during sleep. A sleeping man can be awakened by a noise, and when awake will be frequently able to trace his dream to the impression caused by the noise. This fact seems to prove conclusively the brain's activity during sleep.

A. A mechanical activity certainly ; if under such circumstances there is the slightest perception, or the least glimpse of the dream state, memory comes into play, and the dream can be reconstructed. In the discussion on dreams, the dream state passing into the waking state was compared to the embers of a dying fire ; we may very well continue the simile, and compare the play of the memory to a current of air re-kindling them. That is to say that the waking consciousness recalls to activity the cerebellum, which was fading below the threshold of consciousness.

Q. But does the cerebellum ever cease functioning?

A. No ; but it is lost in the functions of the cerebrum.

Q. That is to say that the stimuli which proceed from the cerebellum during waking life fall below the threshold of waking consciousness, the field of consciousness being entirely occupied by the cerebrum, and this continues till sleep supervenes, when the stimuli from the cerebellum begin in their turn to form the field of consciousness. It is not, therefore, correct to say that the cerebrum is the only seat of consciousness.

A. Quite so ; the function of the cerebrum is to polish, perfect, or co-ordinate ideas, whereas that of the cerebellum produces conscious desires, and so on.

Q. Evidently we have to extend our idea of consciousness. For instance, there is no reason why a sensitive plant should not have consciousness. Du Prel, in his "Philosophie der Mystik," cites some very curious experiments showing a kind of local consciousness, perhaps a kind of reflex connection. He even goes further than this, demonstrating, from a large number of well authenticated cases, such as those of clairvoyants, who can perceive by the pit of the stomach, that the threshold of consciousness is capable of a very wide extension, far wider than we are accustomed to give to it, both upwards and downwards.

A. We may congratulate ourselves on the experiments of Du Prel as an antidote to the theories of Professor Huxley, which are absolutely irreconcileable with the teachings of occultism.

III.

Meeting held at 17, Lansdowne Road, London, W., on January 24th, 1889; Mr. T. B. Harbottle *in the chair.*

STANZA I. *(continued).*

Sloka (5).—DARKNESS ALONE FILLED THE BOUNDLESS ALL, FOR FATHER, MOTHER, AND SON WERE ONCE MORE ONE, AND THE SON HAD NOT AWAKENED YET FOR THE NEW WHEEL AND HIS PILGRIMAGE THEREON.

Q. Is " Darkness" the same as the " Eternal Parent Space" spoken of in Sloka (1) ?

A. Not at all. Here "the boundless all" is the "Parent Space;" and Cosmic Space is something already with attributes, at least potentially. "Darkness," on the other hand, and in this instance, is that of which no attributes can be postulated : it is the Unknown Principle filling Cosmic Space.

Q. Is Darkness, then, used in the sense of the opposite pole to Light?

A. Yes, in the sense of the Unmanifested and the Unknown as the opposite pole to manifestation, and that which falls under the possibility of speculation.

Q. Darkness is not opposed to Light, then, but to differentiation; or rather, may it not be taken as the symbol of Negativeness?

A. The "Darkness" here meant can be opposed to neither Light nor Differentiation, as both are the legitimate effects of the Manvantaric evolution—the cycle of Activity. It is the "Darkness upon the face of the Deep," in *Genesis:* Deep being here " the bright son of the Dark Father " —Space.

Q. Is it that there is no Light or simply nothing to manifest, and no one to perceive it?

A. Both. In the sense of objectivity, both light and darkness are illusions—*maya;* in this case, it is not Darkness as absence of Light, but as one incomprehensible primordial Principle, which, being Absoluteness itself, has for our intellectual perceptions neither form, colour, substantiality, nor anything that could be expressed by words.

Q. When does Light proceed from that Darkness?

A. Subsequently, when the first hour for manifestation strikes.

Q. Light, then, is the first manifestation?

A. It is, after differentiation has begun and at the third stage of evolution only. Bear in mind that in philosophy we use the word "light" in a dual sense: one to signify eternal, absolute light, *in potentia*, ever present in the bosom of the unknown Darkness, coexistent and coeval with the latter in Eternity, or in other words, identical with it; and the other as a Manifestation of heterogeneity and a contrast to it. For one who reads the Vishnu Purâna, for instance, understandingly, will find the differance between the two terms well expressed in Vishnu; one with Brahmâ, and yet distinct from him. There, Vishnu is the eternal x, and at the same time every term of the equation. He is Brahma (neuter) essentially matter and Spirit, which are Brahma's two primordial aspects —Spirit being the abstract light.* In the Vedas, however, we find Vishnu held in small esteem, and no mention made whatever of Brahmâ (the male.)

Q. What is the meaning of the sentence, " Father, Mother and Son were once more one"?

A. It means that the three Logoi—the unmanifested "Father," the semi-manifested "Mother" and the Universe, which is the third *Logos* of our philosophy or Brahmâ, were during the (periodical) *pralaya* once

---

* In the second chapter of the Vishnu Purâna (Wilson's translation) we read—"Parasâra said: Glory to the unchangeable, holy, eternal supreme Vishnu, of one universal nature, the mighty over all: to him who is Hiranyagarbha, Hari, and Sankara, the creator, preserver, and destroyer of the world; to Vâsudeva, the liberator of his worshippers: to him whose essence is both single and manifold; who is both subtile and corporeal, indiscrete and discrete; to Vishnu the cause of final emancipation. Glory to the Supreme Vishnu the cause of the creation, existence, and end of this world; who is the root of the world, and who consists of the world."

And again: "Who can describe him who is not to be apprehended by the senses: who is the best of all things; the supreme soul, self-existent: who is devoid of all the distinguishing characteristics of complexion, caste, or the like; and is exempt from birth, vicissitude, death or decay: who is always and alone: who exists everywhere, and in whom all things here exist; and who is thence named named Vasudeva? He is Brahma (neuter), supreme, lord, eternal, unborn, imperishable, undecaying; of one essence; ever pure, as free from defects. He, that Brahma was (is) all things; comprehending in his own nature the indiscrete and discrete,"

more *one;* differentiated essence had rebecome undifferentiated. The sentence, "Father, Mother, and Son," is the antitype of the Christian type—Father, Son, and Holy Ghost—the last of which was, in early Christianity and Gnosticism, the female "Sophia." It means that all creative and sensitive forces and the effects of such forces which constitute the universe had returned to their primordial state: *all* was merged into one. During the Mahapralayas naught but the Absolute is.

Q. What are the different meanings of Father, Mother and Son? In the Commentary, they are explained as (a) Spirit, Substance and Universe, (b) Spirit, Soul and Body, (c) Universe, Planetary Chain and Man.

A. I have just completed it with my extra definition, which is clear, I think. There is nothing to be added to this explanation, unless we begin to anthropomorphise abstract conceptions.

Q. Taking the last terms of the three series, do the ideas Son, Universe, Man, Body correspond with one another?

A. Of course they do.

Q. And are these terms produced from the remaining pair of terms of each trinity; for instance, the Son from the Father and Mother, the men from the Chain and the Universe, etc., etc., and finally in Pralaya is the Son merged back again into its parents?

A. Before the question is answered, you must be reminded that the period preceding so-called Creation is not spoken about; but only that when matter had begun to differentiate, but had not yet assumed form. Father-Mother is a compound term which means primordial Substance or Spirit-matter. When from Homogeneity it begins through differentiation to fall into Heterogeneity, it becomes positive and negative; thus from the "Zero-state" (or *layam*) it becomes active and passive, instead of the latter alone; and, in consequence of this differentiation (the resultant of which is evolution and the subsequent Universe),—the "Son" is produced, the Son being that same Universe, or manifested Kosmos, till a new *Mahapralaya*.

Q. Or—the ultimate state in layam, *or in the zero point, as in the beginning before the stage of the Father, Mother and Son?*

A. There is but slight reference to that which was before the Father-Mother period in the *Secret Doctrine*. If there is Father-Mother, there can, of course, be no such condition as Laya.

Q. Father, Mother are therefore later than the Laya condition?

A. Quite so; individual objects may be in Laya, but the Universe cannot be so when Father-Mother appears.

Q. Is Fohat one of the three, Father, Mother and Son?

A. Fohat is a generic term and used in many senses. He is the *light* (Daiviprakriti) of all the three *logoi*—the personified symbols of the three *spiritual stages* of Evolution. Fohat is the aggregate of all the spiritual creative ideations *above*, and of all the electro-dynamic and creative forces *below*, in Heaven and on Earth. There seems to be great confusion and misunderstanding concerning the First and Second Logos. The first is the already present yet still unmanifested potentiality in the bosom of Father-Mother; the Second is the abstract collectivity of creators called "Demiurgi" by the Greeks or the Builders of the Universe. The *third logos* is the ultimate differentiation of the Second and the individualization of Cosmic Forces, of which Fohat is the chief; for Fohat is the synthesis of the Seven Creative Rays or Dhyan Chohans which proceed from the third Logos.

Q. During Manvantara when the Son is in existence or awake, does the Father-Mother exist independently or only as manifested in the Son?

A. In using the terms Father, Mother, and Son, we should be on our guard against anthropomorphising the conception; the two former are simply centrifugal and centripetal forces and their product is the "Son"; moreover, it is impossible to exclude either of these factors from the conception in the Esoteric Philosophy.

Q. If so then comes this other point: it is possible to conceive of centripetal and centrifugal forces existing independently of the effects they produce. The effects are always regarded as secondary to the cause or causes.

A. But it is very doubtful whether such a conception can be maintained in, and applied to, our Symbology; if these forces exist they must be producing effects, and if the effects cease, the forces cease with them, for who can know of them?

Q. But they exist as separate entities for mathematical purposes, do they not?

A. That is a different thing; there is a great difference between nature and science, reality and philosophical symbolism. For the same reason we divide man into seven principles, but this does not mean that he has, as it were, seven skins, or entities, or souls. These principles are all aspects of one principle, and even this principle is but a temporary and periodical ray of the One eternal and infinite Flame or Fire.

Sloka (6). THE SEVEN SUBLIME LORDS AND THE SEVEN TRUTHS HAD CEASED TO BE, AND THE UNIVERSE, THE SON OF NECESSITY, WAS IMMERSED IN PARANISHPANNA (*absolute perfection, Paranirvana, which is Yong-Grüb*), TO BE OUTBREATHED BY THAT WHICH IS AND YET IS NOT. NAUGHT WAS.

Sloka (7). THE CAUSES OF EXISTENCE HAD BEEN DONE AWAY WITH; THE VISIBLE THAT WAS, AND THE INVISIBLE THAT IS, RESTED IN ETERNAL NON-BEING, THE ONE BEING.

Q. If the "Causes of existence" had been done away with, how did they come again into existence? It is stated in the Commentary that the chief cause of existence is "the desire to exist," but in the sloka, the universe is called the "son of necessity."

A. "The causes of existence had been done away with" refers to the last Manvantara, or age of Brahmâ, but the cause which makes the Wheel of Time and Space run into Eternity, which is out of Space and Time, has nothing to do with finite causes or what we call Nidânas. There seems to me no contradiction in the statements.

Q. There certainly is a contrast. If the causes of existence had been done away with, how did they come into existence again? But the answer removes the difficulty, for it is stated that one Manvantara had disappeared into Pralaya, and that the cause which led the previous Manvantara to exist is now behind the limits of Space and Time, and therefore causes another Manvantara to come into being.

A. Quite so. This one eternal and therefore, "causeless cause" is immutable and has nothing to do with the causes on any of the planes which are concerned with finite and conditioned being. The cause can therefore by no means be a finite consciousness or desire. It is an absurdity to postulate desire or necessity of the Absolute; the striking of a clock does not suggest the desire of the clock to strike.

Q. But the clock is wound up, and needs a Winder?

A. The same may be said of the universe and this cause, the Absolute containing both clock and Winder, once it is the Absolute ; the only difference is that the former is wound up in Space and Time and the latter out of Space and Time, that is to say in Eternity.

Q. The question really requests an explanation of the cause, in the Absolute, of differentiation?

A. That is outside the province of legitimate speculation. Parabrahm is not a cause, neither is there any cause that can compel it to emanate or create. Strictly speaking, Parabrahm is not even the Absolute but *Absoluteness*. Parabrahm is not the cause, but the causality, or the propelling but not volitional power, in every manifesting Cause. We may have some hazy idea that there is such a thing as this eternal Causeless Cause or Causality. But to define it is impossible. In the *" Lectures on the Bhagavat Gîta,"* by Mr. Subba Row, it is stated that logically even the First Logos cannot cognize Parabrahm, but only Mulaprakriti, its veil. When, therefore, we have yet no clear idea of Mulaprakriti, the first basic aspect of Parabrahm, what can we know of that Supreme Total which is veiled by *Mulaprakriti* (the root of nature or Prakriti) even to the Logos.

Q. What is the meaning of the expression in sloka (7), " the visible that was, and the invisible that is" ?

A. " The visible that was " means the universe of the past Manvantara which had passed into Eternity and was no more. " The invisible that is " signifies the eternal, ever-present and ever-invisible deity, which we call by many names, such as abstract Space, Absolute Sat, etc., and know, in reality, nothing about it.

Sloka (8). ALONE THE ONE FORM OF EXISTENCE STRETCHED, BOUNDLESS, INFINITE, CAUSELESS, IN DREAMLESS SLEEP; AND LIFE PULSATED UNCONSCIOUS IN UNIVERSAL SPACE, THROUGHOUT THAT ALL-PRESENCE WHICH IS SENSED BY THE "OPENED EYE" OF THE DANGMA.

Q. Does the " Eye " open upon the Absolute : or are the " one form of existence" and the "All-Presence" other than the Absolute, or various names for the same Principle.

A. It is all one, of course; simply metaphorical expressions. Please notice that the "Eye" is not said to "*see*"; it only "sensed" the "All-Presence."

Q. *It is through this "Eye" then, that we receive such sense, or feeling, or consciousness?*

A. Through that "Eye," most decidedly; but then one must have such an "Eye" before he can see, or become a *Dangma*, or a Seer.

Q. *The highest spiritual faculty, presumably?*

A. Very well; but where, at that stage, was the happy possessor of it? There was no Dangma to sense the "All-Presence," because there were as yet no men.

Q. *With reference to sloka (6), it was stated that the cause of Light was Darkness?*

A. Darkness has, here again, to be read in a metaphorical sense. It is Darkness most unquestionably to our intellect, inasmuch as we can know nothing of it. I told you already that neither Darkness nor Light are to be used in the sense of opposites, as in the differentiated world. Darkness is the term which will give rise to least misconceptions. For instance, if the term "Chaos" were used, it would be liable to be confounded with chaotic matter.

Q. *The term light was, of course, never used for physical light?*

A. Of course not. Here light is the first potentiality awakening from its *laya* condition to become a potency; it is the first flutter in undifferentiated matter which throws it into objectivity and into a plane from which will start manifestation.

Q. *Later on in the "Secret Doctrine," it is stated that light is made visible by darkness, or rather that darkness exists originally, and that light is the result of the presence of objects to reflect it, that is of the objective world. Now if we take a globe of water and pass an electric beam through it, we shall find that this beam is invisible, unless there are opaque particles in the water, in which case, specks of light will be seen. Is this a good analogy?*

A. It is a very fair illustration, I believe.

Q. *Is not Light a differentiation of vibration?*

A. So we are told in Science; and Sound is also. And so we see that the senses are to a certain extent interchangeable. How would you account, for instance, for the fact that in trance a clairvoyant can read a letter, sometimes placed on the forehead, at the soles of the feet, or on the stomach-pit ?

Q. That is an extra sense.

A. Not at all; it is simply that the sense of seeing can be interchanged with the sense of touch.

Q. But is not the sense of perception the beginning of the sixth sense?

A. That is going beyond the present case, which is simply the interchanging of the senses of touch and sight. Such clairvoyants, however, will not be able to tell the contents of a letter which they have not seen or been brought into contact with ; this requires the exercise of the sixth sense, the former is an exercise of senses on the physical plane, the latter of a sense on a higher plane.

Q. It seems very probable from physiology that every sense may be resolved into the sense of touch, which may be called the co-ordinating sense. This deduction is made from embryological research, which shows that the sense of touch is the first and primary sense, and that all the rest are evolved from it. All the senses, therefore, are more highly specialised or differentiated forms of touch.

A. This is not the view of Eastern philosophy; in the *Anugita*, we read of a conversation between "Brahman" and his wife concerning the senses, seven are spoken of, "mind and understanding" being the other two, according to Mr. Trimbak Telang and Professor Max Müller's translation ; these terms, however, do not convey the correct meaning of the Sanskrit terms. Now, the first sense, according to the Hindus, is connected with sound. This can hardly be the sense of touch.

Q. By touch most probably sensibility, or some sense medium, is meant?

A. In the Eastern philosophy, however, the sense of sound is first manifested, and next the sense of sight, sounds passings into colours. Clairvoyants can *see* sounds and detect every note and modulation far more distinctly than they would by the ordinary sense of sound—vibration, or hearing.

Q. Is it, then, that sound is perceived as a sort of rhythmic movement?

A. Yes ; and such vibrations can be seen at a greater distance than they can be heard.

Q. But supposing the physical hearing were stopped, and a person perceived sounds clairvoyantly, could not this sensation be translated into clairaudience as well?

A. One sense must certainly merge at some point into the other. So also sound can be translated into taste. There are sounds which taste exceedingly acid in the mouths of some sensitives, while others generate the taste of sweetness, in fact, the whole scale of senses is susceptible of correlations.

Q. Then there must be the same extension of the sense of smell?

A. Very naturally, as has been already shown before. The senses are interchangeable once we admit correlation. Moreover they can all be intensified or modified very considerably. You will now understand the reference in the *Vedas* and *Upanishads*, where sounds are said to be perceived.

Q. There was a curious story in the last number of Harper's Magazine of a tribe on an island in the South Seas which have virtually lost the art and habit of speaking and conversing. Yet, they appeared to understand one another and see plainly what each other thought.

A. Such a "Palace of Truth" would hardly suit modern society. However, it was by just such means that the early races are said to have communicated with one another, thought taking an objective form, before speech developed into a distinct spoken language. If so, then there must have been a period in the evolution of the human races when the whole Humanity was composed of sensitives and clairvoyants.

IV.

Meeting held at 17, Lansdowne Road, London, W., on January 31st, 1889;
MR. T. B. HARBOTTLE *in the chair.*

STANZA I. (*continued*).

Q. With reference to sloka (6), where it speaks of the "Seven Lords," since confusion is apt to arise as to the correct application of the terms, what is the distinction between Dhyan-Chohans, Planetary Spirits, Builders and Dhyani-Buddhas?

A. As an additional two volumes of the *Secret Doctrine* would be required to explain all the Hierarchies; therefore, much relating to them has been omitted from the Stanzas and Commentaries. A short definition may, however, be tried. Dhyan-Chohan is a generic term for all Devas, or celestial beings. A Planetary Spirit is a Ruler of a planet, a kind of finite or personal god. There is a marked difference, however, between the Rulers of the Sacred Planets and the Rulers of a small "chain" of worlds like our own. It is no serious objection to say that the earth has, nevertheless, six invisible companions and four different planes, as every other planet, for the difference between them is vital in many a point. Say what one may, our Earth was never numbered among the seven *sacred* planets of the ancients, though in exoteric, popular astrology it stood as a substitute for a secret planet now lost to astronomy, yet well known to initiated specialists. Nor were the Sun or the Moon in that number, though accepted in our day by modern astrology; for the Sun is a Central *Star*, and the Moon a dead planet.

Q. Were none of the six globes of the "terrene" chain numbered among the sacred planets?

A. None. The latter were all planets on *our* plane, and some of them have been discovered later.

Q. Can you tell us something of the planets for which the Sun and the Moon were substitutes?

A. There is no secret in it, though our modern astrologers are ignorant of these planets. One is an intra-mercurial planet, which is supposed to have been discovered, and named by anticipation Vulcan, and the other a planet with a retrograde motion, sometimes visible at a certain hour of night and apparently near the moon. The occult influence of this planet is transmitted by the moon.

Q. *What is it that made these planets sacred or secret?*

A. Their occult influences, as far as I know.

Q. *Then do the Planetary Spirits of the Seven Sacred Planets belong to another hierarchy than to that of the earth?*

A. Evidently; since the terrestial spirit of the earth is not of a very high grade. It must be remembered that the planetary spirit has nothing to do with the spiritual man, but with things of matter and cosmic beings. The gods and rulers of our Earth are cosmic Rulers; that is to say, they form into shape and fashion cosmic matter, for which they were called *Cosmocratores*. They never had any concern with spirit; the Dhyani-Buddhas, belonging to quite a different hierarchy, are especially concerned with the latter.

Q. *These seven Planetary Spirits have therefore nothing really to do with the earth except incidentally?*

A. On the contrary, the " Planetary "—who are not the Dhyani Buddhas—have everything to do with the earth, physically and morally. It is they who rule its destinies and the fate of men. They are Karmic agencies.

Q. *Have they anything to do with the fifth principle—the higher Manas?*

A. No: they have no concern with the three higher principles; they have, however, something to do with the fourth. To recapitulate, therefore; the term " Dhyan-Chohan" is a generic name for all celestial beings. The " Dhyani-Buddhas " are concerned with the human higher triad in a mysterious way that need not be explained here. The " Builders " are a class called, as I already explained, *Cosmocratores*, or the invisible but intelligent Masons, who fashion matter according to the ideal plan ready for them in that which we call Divine and Cosmic Ideation. They were called by the early Masons the " Grand Architect of the Universe " *collectively*: but now the modern Masons make of their G.A.O.T.U. a personal and singular Deity.

Q. Are they not also Planetary Spirits?

A. In a sense they are—as the Earth is also a Planet—but of a lower order.

Q. Do they act under the guidance of the Terrestrial Planetary Spirit?

A. I have just said that they were collectively that Spirit themselves. I wish you to understand that they are not an Entity, a kind of a personal God, but Forces of nature acting under one immutable Law, on the nature of which it is certainly useless for us to speculate.

Q. But are there not Builders of Universes, and Builders of Systems, as there are Builders of our earth?

A. Assuredly there are.

Q. Then the terrestrial Builders are a Planetary "Spirit" like the rest of them, only inferior in kind?

A. I would certainly say so.

Q. Are they inferior according to the size of the planet or inferior in quality?

A. The latter, as we are taught. You see the ancients lacked our modern, and especially theological, conceit, which makes of this little speck of mud of ours something ineffably grander than any of the stars and planets known to us. If, for instance, Esoteric Philosophy teaches that the "Spirit" (collectively again) of Jupiter is far superior to the Terrestrial Spirit, it is not because Jupiter is so many times larger than our earth, but because its substance and texture are so much finer than, and superior to, that of the earth. And it is in proportion to this quality that the Hierarchies of respective "Planetary Builders" reflect and act upon the ideations they find planned for them in the Universal Consciousness, the real great Architect of the Universe.

Q. The Soul of the World, or "Anima Mundi"?

A. Call it so, if you like. It is the Antitype of these Hierarchies, which are its differentiated types. The one *impersonal* Great Architect of the Universe is MAHAT, the Universal Mind. And Mahat is a symbol, an abstraction, an aspect which assumed a hazy, entitative form in the all-materializing conceptions of men.

Q. What is the real difference between the Dhyani-Buddhas in the orthodox and the esoteric conceptions?

A. A very great one philosophically. They are—as higher Devas—called by the Buddhists, Bôdhisatvas. Exoterically they are five in number, whereas in the esoteric schools they are seven, and not single, Entities but *Hierarchies*. It is stated in the *Secret Doctrine* that five Buddhas have come and that two are to come in the sixth and seventh races. Exoterically their president is Vajrasattva, the " Supreme Intelligence " or " Supreme Buddha," but more transcendant still is Vajradhara, even as Parabrahm transcends Brahmâ or Mahat. Thus the exoteric and occult significations of the Dhyani-Buddhas are entirely different. Exoterically each is a trinity, three in one, all three manifesting simultaneously in three worlds—as a human Buddha on earth, a Dhyani-Buddha in the world of astral forms, and an arupa, or formless, Buddha in the highest Nirvanic realm. Thus for a human Buddha, an incarnation of one of these Dhyanis, the stay on earth is limited from seven to seven thousand years in various bodies, since as men they are subjected to normal conditions, accidents and death. In Esoteric philosophy, on the other hand, this means that only five out of the " Seven Dhyani-Buddhas " —or, rather, the Seven Hierarchies of these Dhyanis, who, in Buddhist mysticism, are identical with the higher incarnating Intelligences, or the Kumâras of the Hindus—five only have hitherto appeared on earth in regular succession of incarnations, the last two having to come during the sixth and seventh Root-Races. This is, again, semi-allegorical, if not entirely so. For the sixth and seven Hierarchies have been already incarnated on this earth together with the rest. But as they have reached " Buddhaship," so called, almost from the beginning of the fourth Root-Race, they are said to rest since then in conscious bliss and freedom till the beginning of the Seventh Round, when they will lead Humanity as a new race of Buddhas. These Dhyanis are connected only with Humanity, and, strictly speaking, only with the highest " principles " of men.

Q. Do the Dhyani-Buddhas and the Planetary Spirits in charge of the globes go into pralaya when their planets enter that state ?

A. Only at the end of the seventh Round, and not between each round, for they have to watch over the working of the laws during these minor pralayas. Fuller details on this subject have already been written in the third volume of the *Secret Doctrine*. But all these differences in fact are merely functional, for they are all aspects of one and the same Essence.

Q. Does the hierarchy of Dhyanis, whose province it is to watch over a Round, watch during its period of activity, over the whole series of globes, or only over a particular globe ?

A. There are incarnating and there are watching Dhyanis. Of the functions of the former you have just been told; the latter appear to do their work in this wise. Every class or hierarchy corresponds to one of the Rounds, the first and lowest hierarchy to the first and less developed Round, the second to the second, and so on till the seventh Round is reached, which is under the supervision of the highest Hierarchy of the Seven Dhyanis. At the last, they will appear on earth, as also will some of the Planetary, for the whole humanity will have become Bodhisattvas, their own "sons," *i.e.*, the "Sons" of their own Spirit and Essence or— themselves. Thus there is only a functional difference between the Dhyanis and the Planetary. The one are entirely divine, the other *sidereal*. The former only are called *Anupadaka*, parentless, because they radiated directly from that which is neither Father nor Mother but the unmanifested Logos. They are, in fact, the spiritual aspect of the seven Logoi; and the Planetary Spirits are in their totality, as the seven Sephiroth (the three higher being supercosmic abstractions and *blinds* in the Kabala), and constitute the Heavenly man, or Adam Kadmon; *Dhyani* is a generic name in Buddhism, an abbreviation for all the gods. Yet it must be ever remembered that though they are "gods," still they are not to be worshipped.

Q. Why not, if they are gods?

A. Because Eastern philosophy rejects the idea of a personal and extra-cosmic deity. And to those who call this *atheism*, I would say the following. It is illogical to worship one such god, for, as said in the Bible, "There be Lords many and Gods many." Therefore, *if* worship is desirable, we have to choose either the worship of many gods, each being no better or less limited than the other, viz., polytheism and idolatry, or choose, as the Israelites have done, one tribal or racial god from among them, and while believing in the existence of many gods, ignore and show contempt for the others, regarding our own as the highest and the "God of Gods." But this is logically unwarrantable, for such a god can be neither infinite nor absolute, but must be finite, that is to say, limited and conditioned by space and time. With the Pralaya the tribal god disappears, and Brahmâ and all the other Devas, and the gods are merged into the Absolute. Therefore, occultists do not worship or offer prayers to them, because if we did, we should have either to worship many gods, or pray to the Absolute, which, having no attributes, can have no ears to hear us. The worshipper even of many gods must of necessity be unjust to all the other gods; however far he extends his worship it is simply impossible for him to worship each severally; and in his ignorance, if he choose out any one in particular, he may by no means select the most perfect. Therefore, he would do better far to remember that every man has a god within, a direct ray from the Absolute, the celestial ray from the One; that he has his "god" *within*, not outside, of himself.

Q. Is there any name that can be applied to the planetary Hierarchy or spirit, which watches over the entire evolution of our own globe, such as Brahmâ for instance?

A. None, except the generic name, since it is a septenary and a Hierarchy; unless, indeed, we call it as some Kabalists do—"the Spirit of the Earth."

Q. It is very difficult to remember all these infinite Hierarchies of gods.

A. Not more so than to a chemist to remember the endless symbols of chemistry, if he is a Specialist. In India, alone, however, there are over 300 millions of gods and goddesses. The Manus and Rishis are also planetary gods, for they are said to have appeared at the beginning of the human races to watch over their evolution, and to have incarnated and descended on earth subsequently in order to teach mankind. Then, there are the *Sapta Rishis*, the "Seven Rishis," said exoterically to reside in the constellation of the Great Bear. There are also planetary gods.

Q. Are they higher than Brahmâ?

A. It depends in what aspect one views Brahmâ. In esoteric philosophy he is the synthesis of the seven *logoi*. In exoteric theology he is an aspect of Vishnu with the Vaishnevas, with others something else, as in the *Trimurti*, the Hindu Trinity, he is the chief creator, whereas Vishnu is the Preserver, and Siva the Destroyer. In the Kabala he is certainly Adam Kadmon—the "male-female" man of the first chapter of *Genesis*. For the Manus proceed from Brahmâ as the Sephiroth proceed from Adam Kadmon, and they are also *seven* and *ten*, as circumstances require.

But we may just as well pass on to another Sloka of the Stanzas you want explained.

Sloka (9).—BUT WHERE WAS THE DANGMA WHEN THE ALAYA OF THE UNIVERSE (*Soul as the basis of all, Anima Mundi*) WAS IN PARAMARTHA (*Absolute Being and Consciousness which are Absolute Non-Being and Unconsciousness*) AND THE GREAT WHEEL WAS ANUPADAKA

Q. Does "Alaya" mean that which is never manifested and dissolved, and is it derived from "a," the negative particle, and "laya"?

A. If it is so etymologically—and I am certainly not prepared to answer you one way or the other—it would mean the reverse, since *laya* itself is just that which is not manifested; therefore it would signify *that which is not unmanifested* if anything. Whatever may be the etymological vivisection of the word, it is simply the "Soul of the World," *Anima Mundi*. This is shown by the very wording of the Sloka, which speaks of Alaya being in *Paramartha—i.e.*, in Absolute Non-Being and Unconsciousness, being at the same time absolute perfection or Absoluteness itself. This word, however, is the bone of contention between the Yogacharya and the Madhyamika schools of Northern Buddhism. The scholasticism of the latter makes of *Paramartha (Satya)* something dependent on, and, therefore, relative to other things, thereby vitiating the whole metaphysical philosophy of the word Absoluteness. The other school very rightly denies this interpretation.

Q. Does not the Esoteric Philosophy teach the same doctrines as the Yogacharya School?

A. Not quite. But let us go on.

STANZA II.

Sloka (1)...... WHERE WERE THE BUILDERS, THE LUMINOUS SONS OF MANVANTARIC DAWN?..... IN THE UNKNOWN DARKNESS, IN THEIR AH-HI (*Chohanic, Dhyani-Bhuddic*) PARANISHPANNA, THE PRODUCERS OF FORM (*rupa*) FROM NO-FORM (*arupa*), THE ROOT OF THE WORLD — THE DEVAMATRI AND SVÂBHÂVAT, RESTED IN THE BLISS OF NON-BEING.

Q. Are the "luminous sons of manvantaric dawn" perfected human spirits of the last Manvantara, or are they on their way to humanity in this or a subsequent Manvantara?

A. In this case, which is that of a *Maha*-manvantara after a *Maha*-pralaya, they are the latter. They are the primordial seven rays from which will emanate in their turn all the other luminous and non-luminous lives, whether Archangels, Devils, men or apes. Some have been and some will only now become human beings. It is only after the differentiation of the seven rays and after the seven forces of nature have taken them in hand and worked upon them, that they become cornerstones, or rejected pieces of clay. Everything, therefore, is in these seven rays, but it is impossible to say at this stage in which, because they are not yet differentiated and individualized.

Q. In the following passage :—

" The ' Builders,' the ' Sons of Manvantaric Dawn,' are the real creators of the Universe ; and in this doctrine, which deals only with our Planetary System, they, as the architects of the latter, are also called the ' Watchers ' of the Seven Spheres, which exoterically are the seven planets, and esoterically the seven earths or spheres (planets) of our chain also."

By planetary system is the solar system meant or the chain to which our earth belongs ?

A. The Builders are those who build and fashion things into a form. The term is equally applied to the Builders of the Universe and to the small globes like those of our chain. By planetary system our solar system alone is meant.

Sloka (2). WHERE WAS SILENCE ? WHERE WERE THE EARS TO SENSE IT ? NO! THERE WAS NEITHER SILENCE NOR SOUND.

Q. With reference to the following passage :—

" The idea that things can cease to exist and still BE, is a fundamental one in Eastern psychology. Under the apparent contradiction in terms, there rests a fact in Nature to realize which in the mind, rather than to argue about words is the important thing. A familiar instance of a similar paradox is afforded by chemical combination. The question whether Hydrogen and Oxygen cease to exist, when they combine to form water, is still a moot one."*

Would it be correct to say that what we perceive is a different " element " of the same substance ? For example, when a substance is in the gaseous state, could we say that it is the element Air which is perceived, and that when combined to form water, oxygen and hydrogen appear under the guise of the Element Water, and when in the solid state, ice, we then perceive the element Earth ?

A. The ignorant judge of all things by their appearance and not by what they are in reality. On this earth, of course, water is an element quite distinct from any other element, using the latter term in the sense

---

* S. D., I., 54.

of different manifestations of the one element. The root elements, Earth, Water, Air, Fire, are far more comprehensive states of differentiation. Such being the case, in Occultism Transubstantiation becomes a possibility, seeing that nothing which exists is in reality that which it is supposed to be.

Q. But oxygen which is usually found in its gaseous state, may be liquified and even solidified. When oxygen, then, is found in the gaseous condition, is it the occult element Air which is perceived, and when in the liquid condition the element Water, and in the solid state the element Earth?

A. Most assuredly: we have first of all the Element Fire, not the common fire, but the Fire of the Mediæval Rosicrucians, the one flame, the fire of Life. In differentiation this becomes fire in different aspects. Occultism easily disposes of the puzzle as to whether oxygen and hydrogen cease to exist when combined to form water. Nothing that is in the Universe can disappear from it. For the time being, then, these two gases when combined to form water, are *in abscondito*, but have not ceased to *be*. For, had they been annihilated, Science, by decomposing the water again into oxygen and hydrogen, would have created something out of nothing, and would, therefore, have no quarrel with Theology. Therefore, water is an element, if we choose to call it so, on this plane only. In the same way, oxygen and hydrogen in their turn can be split up into other more subtle elements, all being differentiation of one element or universal essence.

Q. Then all substances on the physical plane are really so many correlations or combinations of these root elements, and ultimately of the one element?

A. Most assuredly. In occultism it is always best to proceed from universals to particulars.

Q. Apparently, then, the whole basis of occultism lies in this, that there is latent within every man a power which can give him true knowledge, a power of perception of truth, which enables him to deal first hand with universals if he will be strictly logical and face the facts. Thus we can proceed from universals to particulars by this innate spiritual force which is in every man.

A. Quite so: this power is inherent in all, but paralyzed by our methods of education, and especially by the Aristotelian and Baconian methods. Hypothesis now reigns triumphant.

Q. It is curious to read Schopenhauer and Hartmann and mark how, step by step, by strict logic and pure reason, they have arrived at the same bases of thought that had been centuries ago adopted in India, especially by the Vedantin System. It may, however, be objected that they have arrived at this by the inductive method. But in Schopenhauer's case at any rate it was not so. He acknowledges himself that the idea came to him like a flash; having thus got his fundamental idea he set to work to arrange his facts, so that the reader imagines that what was in reality an intuitive idea, is a logical deduction drawn from the facts.

A. This is not only true of the Schopenhauerian philosophy, but also of all the great discoveries of modern times. How, for instance, did Newton discover the law of gravity? Was it not by the simple fall of an apple, and not by an elaborate series of experiments. The time will come when the Platonic method will not be so entirely ignored and men will look with favour on methods of education which will enable them to develop this most spiritual faculty.

APPENDIX.

Meetings held at 17, Lansdowne Road, London, W., on December 20th and 27th, 1888; Mr. T. B. HARBOTTLE in the Chair.

[The following is the Summary of the teachings during several meetings which preceded the Transactions of the " Blavatsky Lodge of the T. S.," when the explanations of the *stanzas* from the " Secret Doctrine " became incorporated in a regular series of instructions.]

DREAMS.

Q. What are the " principles " which are active during dreams?

A. The "principles" active during ordinary dreams—which ought to be distinguished from real dreams, and called idle visions—are *Kama*, the seat of the personal Ego and of desire awakened into chaotic activity by the slumbering reminiscences of the lower Manas.

Q. What is the " lower Manas"?

A. It is usually called the animal soul (the *Nephesh* of the Hebrew Kabalists). It is the ray which emanates from the Higher Manas or permanent EGO, and is that " principle " which forms the human mind—in animals instinct, for animals also dream.* The combined action of Kama and the " animal soul," however, are purely mechanical. It is instinct, not reason, which is active in them. During the sleep of the body they receive and send out mechanically electric shocks to and from various nerve-centres. The brain is hardly impressed by them, and memory stores them, of course, without order or sequence. On waking these impressions gradually fade out, as does every fleeting shadow that has no basic or substantial reality underlying it. The retentive faculty of the brain, however, may register and preserve them if they are only impressed strongly enough. But, as a rule, our memory registers only the fugitive and distorted impressions which the brain receives at the moment of awakening. This aspect of "dreams" however, has been sufficiently observed and is described correctly enough in modern physiological and biological works, as such human dreams do not differ much from those of the animals. That which is entirely *terra incognita* for Science is the

---

* The word dream means really "to slumber "—the latter function being called in Russian " *dreamátj.*"—ED.

real dreams and experiences of the higher EGO, which are also called dreams, but ought not to be so termed, or else the term for the other sleeping "visions" changed.

Q. How do these differ?

A. The nature and functions of real dreams cannot be understood unless we admit the existence of an immortal Ego in mortal man, independent of the physical body, for the subject becomes quite unintelligible unless we believe—that which is a fact—that during sleep there remains only an animated form of clay, whose powers of independent thinking are utterly paralyzed.

But if we admit the existence of a higher or permanent *Ego* in us—which Ego must not be confused with what we call the "Higher Self,"—we can comprehend that what we often regard as dreams, generally accepted as idle fancies, are, in truth, stray pages torn out from the life and experiences of the *inner* man, and the dim recollection of which at the moment of awakening becomes more or less distorted by our physical memory. The latter catches mechanically a few impressions of the thoughts, facts witnessed, and deeds performed by the *inner* man during its hours of complete freedom. For our *Ego* lives its own separate life within its prison of clay whenever it becomes free from the trammels of matter, *i.e.*, during the sleep of the physical man. This Ego it is which is the actor, the real man, the true human self. But the physical man cannot feel or be conscious during dreams; for the personality, the outer man, with its brain and thinking apparatus, are paralyzed more or less completely.

We might well compare the real Ego to a prisoner, and the physical personality to the gaoler of his prison. If the gaoler falls asleep, the prisoner escapes, or, at least, passes outside the walls of his prison. The gaoler is half asleep, and looks nodding all the time out of a window, through which he can catch only occasional glimpses of his prisoner, as he would a kind of shadow moving in front of it. But what can he perceive, and what can he know of the real actions, and especially the thoughts, of his charge?

Q. Do not the thoughts of the one impress themselves upon the other?

A. Not during sleep, at all events; for the real Ego does not think as his evanescent and temporary personality does. During the waking hours the thoughts and Voice of the Higher Ego do or do not reach his gaoler —the physical man, for they are the *Voice of his Conscience*, but during his sleep they are absolutely the "Voice in the desert." In the thoughts of the *real* man, or the immortal "Individuality," the pictures and visions of the Past and Future are as the Present; nor are his thoughts like ours, subjective pictures in our cerebration, but living acts and deeds, present actualities. They are realities, even as they were when speech expressed in sounds did not exist; when thoughts were things, and men did not need to express them in speeches; for they instantly realised themselves in action by the power of *Kriya-Sakti*, that mysterious power which transforms instantaneously ideas into visible forms, and these were as objective to the "man" of the early *third* Race as objects of sight are now to us.

Q. How, then, does Esoteric Philosophy account for the transmission of even a few fragments of those thoughts of the Ego to our physical memory which it sometimes retains?

A. All such are reflected on the brain of the sleeper, like outside shadows on the canvas walls of a tent, which the occupier sees as he wakes. Then the man thinks that he has dreamed all that, and feels as though *he* had lived through something, while in reality it is the *thought-actions* of the true Ego which he has dimly perceived. As he becomes fully awake, his recollections become with every minute more distorted, and mingle with the images projected from the physical brain, under the action of the stimulus which causes the sleeper to awaken. These recollections, by the power of association, set in motion various trains of ideas.

Q. It is difficult to see how the Ego can be acting during the night things which have taken place long ago. Was it not stated that dreams are not subjective?

A. How can they be subjective when the dream state is itself for us, and on our plane, at any rate, a subjective one? To the dreamer (the Ego), on his own plane, the things on that plane are as objective to him as our acts are to us.

Q. What are the senses which act in dreams?

A. The senses of the sleeper receive occasional shocks, and are awakened into mechanical action; what he hears and sees are, as has been said, a distorted reflection of the thoughts of the Ego. The latter is highly spiritual, and is linked very closely with the higher principles, Buddhi and Atma. These higher principles are entirely inactive on our plane, and the higher Ego (*Manas*) itself is more or less dormant during the waking of the physical man. This is especially the case with persons of very materialistic mind. So dormant are the Spiritual faculties, because the Ego is so trammelled by matter, that *It* can hardly give all its attention to the man's actions, even should the latter commit sins for which that Ego—when reunited with its *lower* Manas—will have to suffer conjointly in the future. It is, as I said, the impressions projected into the physical man by this Ego which constitute what we call "conscience"; and in proportion as the Personality, the lower Soul (or *Manas*), unites itself to its higher consciousness, or Ego, does the action of the latter upon the life of mortal man become more marked.

Q. This Ego, then, is the "Higher Ego"?

A. Yes; it is the higher Manas illuminated by Buddhi; the principle of self-consciousness, the "I-am-I," in short. It is the Karana-Sarira, the immortal man, which passes from one incarnation to another.

Q. Is the "register" or "tablet of memory" for the true dream-state different from that of waking life?

A. Since dreams are in reality the actions of the Ego during physical sleep, they are, of course, recorded on their own plane and produce their appropriate effects on this one. But it must be always remembered that dreams in general, and as we know them, are simply our waking and hazy recollections of these facts.

It oftens happens, indeed, that we have no recollection of having dreamt at all, but later in the day the remembrance of the dream will suddenly flash upon us. Of this there are many causes. It is analogous to what sometimes happens to every one of us. Often a sensation, a smell, even a casual noise, or a sound, brings instantaneously to our mind long-forgotten events, scenes and persons. Something of what was seen, done, or thought by the "night-performer," the Ego, impressed itself at that time on the physical brain, but was not brought into the conscious, waking memory, owing to some physical condition or obstacle. This impression is registered on the brain in its appropriate cell or nerve centre, but owing to some accidental circumstance it "hangs fire," so to say, till something gives it the needed impulse. Then the brain slips it off immediately into the conscious memory of the waking man; for as soon as the conditions required are supplied, that particular centre starts forthwith into activity, and does the work which it had to do, but was hindered at the time from completing.

Q. How does this process take place?

A. There is a sort of conscious telegraphic communication going on incessantly, day and night, between the physical brain and the inner man. The brain is such a complex thing, both physically and metaphysically, that it is like a tree whose bark you can remove layer by layer, each layer being different from all the others, and each having its own special work, function, and properties.

Q. *What distinguishes the " dreaming" memory and imagination from those of waking consciousness ?*

A. During sleep the physical memory and imagination are of course passive, because the dreamer is asleep : his brain is asleep, his memory is asleep, all his functions are dormant and at rest. It is only when they are stimulated, as I told you, that they are aroused. Thus the consciousness of the sleeper is not active, but passive. The inner man, however, the real Ego, acts independently during the sleep of the body ; but it is doubtful if any of us—unless thoroughly acquainted with the physiology of occultism —could understand the nature of its action.

Q. *What relation have the Astral Light and Akâsa to memory ?*

A. The former is the " tablet of the memory " of the animal man, the latter of the spiritual Ego. The "dreams" of the Ego, as much as the acts of the physical man, are all recorded, since both are actions based on causes and producing results. Our " dreams," being simply the waking state and actions of the true Self, must be, of course, recorded somewhere. Read "Karmic Visions" in *Lucifer*, and note the description of the real Ego, sitting as a spectator of the life of the hero, and perhaps something will strike you.

Q. *What, in reality, is the Astral Light ?*

A. As the Esoteric Philosophy teaches us, the *Astral Light* is simply the dregs of *Akasa* or the Universal Ideation in its metaphysical sense. Though invisible, it is yet, so to speak, the phosphorescent radiation of the latter, and is the medium between it and man's thought-faculties. It is these which pollute the Astral Light, and make it what it is—the storehouse of all human and especially psychic iniquities. In its primordial genesis, the astral light as a radiation is quite pure, though the lower it descends approaching our terrestrial sphere, the more it differentiates, and becomes as a result impure in its very constitution. But man helps considerably to this pollution, and gives it back its essence far worse than when he received it.

Q. Can you explain to us how it is related to man, and its action in dream-life?

A. Differentiation in the physical world is infinite. Universal ideation—or *Mahat*, if you like it—sends its homogeneous radiation into the heterogeneous world, and this reaches the human or *personal* minds through the Astral Light.

Q. But do not our minds receive their illuminations direct from the Higher Manas through the Lower? And is not the former the pure emanation of divine Ideation—the " Manasa-Putras," which incarnated in men?

A. They are. Individual *Manasa-Putras* or the Kumaras are the direct radiations of the divine Ideation—"individual" in the sense of later differentiation, owing to numberless incarnations. In sum they are the collective aggregation of that Ideation, become on our plane, or from our point of view, *Mahat*, as the Dhyan Chohans are in their aggregate the WORD or "Logos" in the formation of the World. Were the Personalities (Lower Manas or the *physical* minds) to be inspired and illumined solely by their higher *alter Egos* there would be little sin in this world. But they are not; and getting entangled in the meshes of the Astral Light, they separate themselves more and more from their parent Egos. Read and study what Eliphas Lévi says of the Astral Light, which he calls Satan and the Great Serpent. The Astral Light has been taken too literally to mean some sort of a second blue sky. This imaginary space, however, on which are impressed the countless images of all that ever was, is, and will be, is but a too sad reality. It becomes in, and for, man—if at all psychic—and who is not?—a tempting Demon, his " evil angel," and the inspirer of all our worst deeds. It acts on the will of even the sleeping man, through visions impressed upon his slumbering brain (which visions must not be confused with the " dreams "), and these germs bear their fruit when he awakes.

Q. What is the part played by Will in dreams?

A. The will of the outer man, our volition, is of course dormant and inactive during dreams; but a certain bent can be given to the slumbering will during its inactivity, and certain after-results developed by the mutual inter-action—produced almost mechanically—through union between two or more "principles" into one, so that they will act in perfect harmony, without any friction or a single false note, when awake. But this is one of the dodges of " black magic," and when used for good purposes belongs to the training of an Occultist. One must be far advanced on the "path" to have a will which can act consciously during his physical sleep, or act on the will of another person during the sleep of the latter, *e.g.*, to control his dreams, and thus control his actions when awake.

Q. We are taught that a man can unite all his "principles" into one—what does this mean?

A. When an adept succeeds in doing this he is a *Jivanmukta*: he is no more of this earth virtually, and becomes a Nirvanee, who can go into *Samadhi* at will. Adepts are generally classed by the number of "principles" they have under their perfect control, for that which we call will has its seat in the higher EGO, and the latter, when it is rid of its sin-laden personality, is divine and pure.

Q. What part does Karma play in dreams? In India they say that every man receives the reward or punishment of all his acts, both in the waking and the dream state.

A. If they say so, it is because they have preserved in all their purity and remembered the traditions of their forefathers. They know that the Self is the *real* Ego, and that it lives and acts, though on a different plane. The external life is a "dream" to this Ego, while the inner life, or the life on what we call the dream plane, is the real life for it. And so the Hindus (the profane, of course) say that Karma is generous, and rewards the real man in dreams as well as it does the false personality in physical life.

Q. What is the difference, "karmically," between the two?

A. The physical animal man is as little responsible as a dog or a mouse. For the bodily form all is over with the death of the body. But the real SELF, that which emanated its own shadow, or the lower thinking personality, that enacted and pulled the wires during the life of the physical automaton, will have to suffer conjointly with its *factotum and alter ego* in its next incarnation.

Q. But the two, the higher and the lower, Manas are one, are they not?

A. They are, and yet they are not—and that is the great mystery. The Higher Manas or EGO is essentially divine, and therefore pure; no stain can pollute it, as no punishment can reach it, *per se*, the more so since it is innocent of, and takes no part in, the deliberate transactions of its Lower Ego. Yet by the very fact that, though dual and during life the Higher is distinct from the Lower, "the Father and Son" *are one*, and because that in reuniting with the parent Ego, the Lower Soul fastens upon and impresses upon it all its bad as well as good actions—both have to suffer, the Higher Ego, though innocent and without blemish, has to bear the punishment of the misdeeds committed by the *lower* Self together with it in their future incarnation. The whole doctrine of atonement is built upon this old esoteric tenet; for the Higher Ego is the antitype of that which is on this earth the type, namely, the personality. It is, for those who understand it, the old Vedic story of Visvakarman over again, practically demonstrated. Visvakarman, the all-seeing Father-God, who is beyond the comprehension of mortals, ends, as son of Bhuvana, the holy Spirit, by *sacrificing himself to himself*, to save the worlds. The mystic name of the "Higher Ego" is, in the Indian philosophy, *Kshetrajna*, or "embodied Spirit," that which knows or informs *kshetra*, "the body." Etymologize the name, and you will find in it the term *aja*, "first-born," and also the "lamb." All this is very suggestive, and volumes might be written upon the pregenetic and postgenetic development of type and antitype—of Christ-*Kshetrajna*, the "God-Man," the First-born, symbolized as the "lamb." The *Secret Doctrine* shows that the Manasa-Putras or incarnating Egos have taken upon themselves, voluntarily and knowingly, the burden of all the future sins of their future personalities. Thence it is easy to see that it is neither Mr. A. nor Mr. B., nor any of the personalities that periodically clothe the Self-Sacrificing Ego, which are the real Sufferers, but verily the innocent *Christos* within us. Hence the mystic Hindus say that the Eternal Self, or the Ego (the one in three and three in one), is the "Charioteer" or driver; the personalities are the temporary and evanescent passengers; while the horses are the animal passions of man. It is, then, true to say that when we remain deaf to the Voice of our Conscience, we crucify the Christos within us. But let us return to dreams.

Q. Are so-called prophetic dreams a sign that the dreamer has strong clairvoyant faculties?

A. It may be said, in the case of persons who have truly prophetic dreams, that it is because their physical brains and memory are in closer relation and sympathy with their "Higher Ego" than in the generality of men. The Ego-Self has more facilities for impressing upon the physical shell and memory that which is of importance to such persons than it has in the case of other less gifted persons. Remember that the only God man comes in contact with is his own God, called Spirit, Soul and Mind, or Consciousness, and these three are one.

But there are weeds that must be destroyed in order that a plant may grow. We must die, said St. Paul, that we may live again. It is through destruction that we may improve, and the three powers, the preserving, the creating and the destroying, are only so many aspects of the divine spark within man.

Q. Do Adepts dream?

A. No advanced Adept dreams. An adept is one who has obtained mastery over his four lower principles, including his body, and does not, therefore, let flesh have its own way. He simply paralyzes his lower Self during Sleep, and becomes perfectly free. A dream, as we understand it, is an illusion. Shall an adept, then, dream when he has rid himself of every other illusion? In his sleep he simply lives on another and more real plane.

Q. Are there people who have never dreamed?

A. There is no such man in the world so far as I am aware. All dream more or less; only with most, dreams vanish suddenly upon waking. This depends on the more or less receptive condition of the brain ganglia. Unspiritual men, and those who do not exercise their imaginative faculties, or those whom manual labour has exhausted, so that the ganglia do not act even mechanically during rest, dream rarely, if ever, with any coherence.

Q. What is the difference between the dreams of men and those of beasts?

A. The dream state is common not only to all men, but also to all animals, of course, from the highest mammalia to the smallest birds, and even insects. Every being endowed with a physical brain, or organs approximating thereto, must dream. Every animal, large or small, has, more or less, physical senses; and though these senses are dulled during sleep, memory will still, so to say, act mechanically, reproducing past sensations. That dogs and horses and cattle dream we all know, and so also do canaries, but such dreams are, I think, merely physiological. Like the last embers of a dying fire, with its spasmodic flare and occasional flames, so acts the brain in falling asleep. Dreams are not, as Dryden says, "interludes which fancy makes," for such can only refer to physiological dreams provoked by indigestion, or some idea or event which has impressed itself upon the active brain during waking hours.

Q. What, then, is the process of going to sleep?

A. This is partially explained by Physiology. It is said by Occultism to be the periodical and regulated exhaustion of the nervous centres, and especially of the sensory ganglia of the brain, which refuse to act any longer on this plane, and, if they would not become unfit for work, are compelled to recuperate their strength on another plane or *Upadhi*. First comes the *Svapna*, or dreaming state, and this leads to that of *Shushupti*. Now it must be remembered that our senses are all dual, and act according to the plane of consciousness on which the thinking entity energises. Physical sleep affords the greatest facility for its action on the various planes; at the same time it is a necessity, in order that the senses may recuperate and obtain a new lease of life for the *Jagrata*, or waking state, from the *Svapna* and *Shushupti*. According to *Raj Yoga*, *Turya* is the highest state. As a man exhausted by one state of the life fluid seeks another; as, for example, when exhausted by the hot air he refreshes himself with cool water; so sleep is the shady nook in the sunlit valley of life. Sleep is a sign that waking life has become too strong for the physical organism, and that the force of the life current must be broken by changing the waking for the sleeping state. Ask a good clairvoyant to describe the aura of a person just refreshed by sleep, and that of another just before going to sleep. The former will be seen bathed in rhythmical vibrations of life currents— golden, blue, and rosy; these are the electrical waves of Life. The latter is, as it were, in a mist of intense golden-orange hue, composed of atoms whirling with an almost incredible spasmodic rapidity, showing that the person begins to be too strongly saturated with Life; the life essence is too strong for his physical organs, and he must seek relief in the shadowy side of that essence, which side is the dream element, or physical sleep, one of the states of consciousness.

Q. But what is a dream?

A. That depends on the meaning of the term. You may "dream," or, as we say, sleep visions, awake or asleep. If the Astral Light is collected in a cup or metal vessel by will-power, and the eyes fixed on some point in it with a strong will to see, a waking vision or "dream" is the result, if the person is at all sensitive. The reflections in the Astral Light are seen better with closed eyes, and, in sleep, still more distinctly. From a lucid state, vision becomes translucid; from normal organic consciousness it rises to a transcendental state of consciousness.

Q. To what causes are dreams chiefly due?

A. There are many kinds of dreams, as we all know. Leaving the "digestion dream" aside, there are brain dreams and memory dreams, mechanical and conscious visions. Dreams of warning and premonition require the active co-operation of the inner Ego. They are also often due to the conscious or unconscious co-operation of the brains of two living persons, or of their two Egos.

Q. What is it that dreams, then?

A. Generally the physical brain of the personal Ego, the seat of memory, radiating and throwing off sparks like the dying embers of a fire. The memory of the Sleeper is like an Æolian seven-stringed harp; and his state of mind may be compared to the wind that sweeps over the chords. The corresponding string of the harp will respond to that one of the seven states of mental activity in which the sleeper was before falling asleep. If it is a gentle breeze the harp will be affected but little; if a hurricane, the vibrations will be proportionately powerful. If the personal Ego is in touch with its higher principles and the veils of the higher planes are drawn aside, all is well; if on the contrary it is of a materialistic animal nature, there will be probably no dreams; or if the memory by chance catch the breath of a "wind" from a higher plane, seeing that it will be impressed through the sensory ganglia of the cerebellum, and not by the direct agency of the spiritual Ego, it will receive pictures and sounds so distorted and inharmonious that even a Devachanic vision would appear a nightmare or grotesque caricature. Therefore there is no simple answer to the question "What is it that dreams," for it depends entirely on each individual what principle will be the chief motor in dreams, and whether they will be remembered or forgotten.

Q. Is the apparent objectivity in a dream really objective or subjective?

A. If it is admitted to be apparent, then of course it is subjective. The question should rather be, to whom or what are the pictures or representations in dreams either objective or subjective? To the physical man, the *dreamer*, all he sees with his eyes shut, and in or through his mind, is of course subjective. But to the *Seer* within the physical dreamer, that Seer himself being subjective to our material senses, all he sees is as objective as he is himself to himself and to others like himself. Materialists will probably laugh, and say that we make of a man a whole family of entities, but this is not so. Occultism teaches that physical man is one, but the thinking man septenary, thinking, acting, feeling, and living on seven different states of being or planes of consciousness, and that for all these states and planes the permanent Ego (not the false personality) has a distinct set of senses.

Q. Can these different senses be distinguished?

A. Not unless you are an Adept or highly-trained Chela, thoroughly acquainted with these different states. Sciences, such as biology, physiology, and even psychology (of the Maudsley, Bain, and Herbert Spencer schools), do not touch on this subject. Science teaches us about the phenomena of volition, sensation, intellect, and instinct, and says that these are all manifested through the nervous centres, the most important of which is our brain. She will speak of the peculiar agent or substance through which these phenomena take place as the vascular and fibrous tissues, and explain their relation to one another, dividing the ganglionic centres into motor, sensory and sympathetic, but will never breathe one word of the mysterious agency of intellect itself, or of the mind and its functions.

Now, it frequently happens that we are conscious and know that we are dreaming; this is a very good proof that man is a multiple being on the thought plane; so that not only is the Ego, or thinking man, Proteus, a multiform, ever-changing entity, but he is also, so to speak, capable of separating himself on the mind or dream plane into two or more entities; and on the plane of illusion which follows us to the threshold of Nirvâna, he is like Ain-Soph talking to Ain-Soph, holding a dialogue with himself and speaking through, about, and to himself. And this is the mystery of the inscrutable Deity in the *Zohar*, as in the Hindu philosophies; it is the same in the Kabbala, Puranas, Vedantic metaphysics, or even in the so-called Christian mystery of the Godhead and Trinity. Man is the microcosm of the macrocosm; the god on earth is built on the pattern of the god in nature. But the universal consciousness of the real Ego transcends a millionfold the self-consciousness of the personal or false Ego.

Q. Is that which is termed "unconscious cerebration" during sleep a mechanical process of the physical brain, or is it a conscious operation of the Ego, the result of which only is impressed on the ordinary consciousness?

A. It is the latter; for is it possible to remember in our conscious state what took place while our brain worked unconsciously? This is apparently a contradiction in terms.

Q. How does it happen that persons who have never seen mountains in nature often see them distinctly in sleep, and are able to note their features?

A. Most probably because they have seen pictures of mountains; otherwise it is somebody or something in us which has previously seen them.

Q. What is the cause of that experience in dreams in which the dreamer seems to be ever striving after something, but never attaining it?

A. It is because the physical self and its memory are shut out of the possibility of knowing what the real Ego does. The dreamer only catches faint glimpses of the doings of the Ego, whose actions produce the so-called dream on the physical man, but is unable to follow it consecutively. A delirious patient, on recovery, bears the same relation to the nurse who watched and tended him in his illness as the physical man to his real Ego. The Ego acts as consciously within and without him as the nurse acts in tending and watching over the sick man. But neither the patient after leaving his sick bed, nor the dreamer on awaking, will be able to remember anything except in snatches and glimpses.

Q. How does sleep differ from death?

A. There is an analogy certainly, but a very great difference between the two. In sleep there is a connection, weak though it may be, between the lower and higher mind of man, and the latter is more or less reflected into the former, however much its rays may be distorted. But once the body is dead, the body of illusion, *Mayavi Rupa*, becomes Kama Rupa, or the animal soul, and is left to its own devices. Therefore, there is as much difference between the spook and man as there is between a gross material, animal but sober mortal, and a man incapably drunk and unable to distinguish the most prominent surroundings; between a person shut up in a perfectly dark room and one in a room lighted, however imperfectly, by some light or other.

The lower principles are like wild beasts, and the higher Manas is the rational man who tames or subdues them more or less successfully. But once the animal gets free from the master who held it in subjection; no sooner has it ceased to hear his voice and see him than it starts off again to the jungle and its ancient den. It takes, however, some time for an animal to return to its original and natural state, but these lower principles or "spook" return instantly, and no sooner has the higher Triad entered the Devachanic state than the lower Duad rebecomes that which it was from the beginning, a principle endued with purely animal instinct, made happier still by the great change.

Q. What is the condition of the Linga Sarira, or plastic body, during dreams?

A. The condition of the Plastic form is to sleep with its body, unless projected by some powerful desire generated in the higher Manas. In dreams it plays no active part, but on the contrary is entirely passive, being the involuntarily half-sleepy witness of the experiences through which the higher principles are passing.

Q. Under what circumstances is this wraith seen?

A. Sometimes, in cases of illness or very strong passion on the part of the person seen or the person who sees; the possibility is mutual. A sick person especially just before death, is very likely to see in dream, or vision, those whom he loves and is continually thinking of, and so also is a person awake, but intensely thinking of a person who is asleep at the time.

Q. Can a Magician summon such a dreaming entity and have intercourse with it?

A. In black Magic it is no rare thing to evoke the "spirit" of a sleeping person; the sorcerer may then learn from the apparition any secret he chooses, and the sleeper be quite ignorant of what is occurring. Under such circumstances that which appears is the *Mayavi rupa*; but there is always a danger that the memory of the living man will preserve the recollections of the evocation and remember it as a vivid dream. If it is not, however, at a great distance, the Double or *Linga Sarira* may be evoked, but this can neither speak nor give information, and there is always the possibility of the sleeper being killed through this forced separation. Many sudden deaths in sleep have thus occurred, and the world been no wiser.

Q. Can there be any connection between a dreamer and an entity in "Kama Loka"?

A. The dreamer of an entity in *Kama Loka* would probably bring upon himself a nightmare, or would run the risk of becoming "possessed" by the "spook" so attracted, if he happened to be a medium, or one who had made himself so passive during his waking hours that even his higher Self is now unable to protect him. This is why the mediumistic state of passivity is so dangerous, and in time renders the Higher Self entirely helpless to aid or even warn the sleeping or entranced person. Passivity paralyzes the connection between the lower and higher principles. It is very rare to find instances of mediums who, while remaining passive *at will*, for the purpose of communicating with some higher Intelligence, some *exterraneous* spirit (not disembodied), will yet preserve sufficiently their personal will so as not to break off all connection with the higher Self.

Q. Can a dreamer be " en rapport" with an entity in Devachan ?

A. The only possible means of communicating with Devachanees is during sleep by a dream or vision, or in trance state. No Devachanee can descend into our plane ; it is for us—or rather our *inner Self*—to ascend to his.

Q. What is the state of mind of a drunkard during sleep ?

A. It is no real sleep, but a heavy stupor ; no physical rest, but worse than sleeplessness, and kills the drunkard as quickly. During such stupor, as also during the waking drunken state, everything turns and whirls round in the brain, producing in the imagination and fancy horrid and grotesque shapes in continual motion and convolutions.

Q. What is the cause of nightmare, and how is it that the dreams of persons suffering from advanced consumption are often pleasant?

A. The cause of the former is simply physiological. A nightmare arises from oppression and difficulty in breathing ; and difficulty in breathing will always create such a feeling of oppression and produce a sensation of impending calamity. In the second case, dreams become pleasant because the consumptive grows daily severed from his material body, and more clairvoyant in proportion. As death approaches, the body wastes away and ceases to be an impediment or barrier between the brain of the physical man and his Higher Self.

Q. Is it a good thing to cultivate dreaming?

A. It is by cultivating the power of what is called "dreaming" that clairvoyance is developed.

Q. Are there any means of interpreting dreams—for instance, the interpretations given in dream-books ?

A. None but the clairvoyant faculty and the spiritual intuition of the "interpreter." Every dreaming Ego differs from every other, as our physical bodies do. If everything in the universe has seven keys to its symbolism on the physical plane, how many keys may it not have on higher planes ?

Q. Is there any way in which dreams may be classified?

A. We may roughly divide also dreams into seven classes, and subdivide these in turn. Thus, we would divide them into :—

1. Prophetic dreams. These are impressed on our memory by the Higher Self, and are generally plain and clear : either a voice heard or the coming event foreseen.

2. Allegorical dreams, or hazy glimpses of realities caught by the brain and distorted by our fancy. These are generally only half true.

3. Dreams sent by adepts, good or bad, by mesmerisers, or by the thoughts of very powerful minds bent on making us do their will.

4. Retrospective; dreams of events belonging to past incarnations.

5. Warning dreams for others who are unable to be impressed themselves.

6. Confused dreams, the causes of which have been discussed above.

7. Dreams which are mere fancies and chaotic pictures, owing to digestion, some mental trouble, or such-like external cause.

Our Complete Catalog

may be obtained by filling out this card and returning it to us.

PLEASE PRINT

Mr/Mrs/Ms ─────────────────────────

Address ─────────────────────────

City, State, & Post Code ─────────────────

Country ─────────────────────────

Please include information about:

☐ The Theosophical Society ☐ Correspondence Courses

Visit us online at www.theosociety.org

Place Stamp Here

THEOSOPHICAL UNIVERSITY PRESS
P O BOX C
PASADENA CA 91109–7107 USA

TRANSACTIONS

OF

THE BLAVATSKY LODGE

OF THE

THEOSOPHICAL SOCIETY.

DISCUSSIONS ON THE STANZAS OF THE FIRST VOLUME

OF

THE SECRET DOCTRINE.

PART II.

STANZAS II TO IV (SLOKAS 1 TO 5).

FEBRUARY AND MARCH, 1889.

London:
THE THEOSOPHICAL PUBLISHING SOCIETY,
7, DUKE STREET, ADELPHI, W.C.

New York:
W. Q. JUDGE, 132, NASSAU STREET,
1891.

All Rights Reserved.

[*The following transactions are compiled from shorthand notes taken at the meetings of the Blavatsky Lodge of the Theosophical Society, from January 10th to June 20th, 1889, being somewhat condensed from the original discussions.*

"*The Secret Doctrine*" *being based upon the archaic stanzas of the* "*Book of Dzyan,*" *and these being too abstruse for most of the new students of Esoteric philosophy, the members of the* "*B. L. of the T. S.*" *agreed to devote the debates of the weekly meetings to each stanza and sundry other metaphysical subjects.*

The questions were put by members who, for the most part, supported their objections and exceptions on modern scientific grounds, and assumed logical deductions based thereon. As such objections are generally the common property of students of "*The Secret Doctrine,*" *it has been judged unnecessary to incorporate them in full so that their substance alone has been retained. The answers in all cases are based on the shorthand Reports, and are those of Esoteric Philosophy as given by H. P. B. herself.*]

V.

Meeting held at 17, *Lansdowne Road, London, W., on February* 7*th*, 1889; MR. W. KINGSLAND *in the chair.*

STANZA II. *(continued.)*

Sloka (3). THE HOUR HAD NOT YET STRUCK? THE RAY HAD NOT YET FLASHED INTO THE GERM; THE MATRI-PADMA *(mother lotus)* HAD NOT YET SWOLLEN.

"The Ray of the 'ever-darkness' becomes, as it is emitted, a ray of effulgent life, and flashes into the 'germ'—the point in the Mundane Egg, represented by matter in its abstract sense."

Q. Is the Point in the Mundane Egg the same as the Point in the Circle, the Unmanifested Logos?

A. Certainly not: the Point in the Circle is the Unmanifested Logos, the Manifested Logos is the Triangle. Pythagoras speaks of the never manifested Monad which lives in solitude and darkness; when the hour strikes it radiates from itself ONE the first number. This number descending, produces Two, the second number, and Two, in its turn, produces THREE, forming a triangle, the first complete geometrical figure in the world of form. It is this ideal or abstract triangle which is the Point in the Mundane Egg, which, after gestation, and in the third remove, will start from the Egg to form the Triangle. This is Brahmâ-Vâch-Virâj in the Hindu Philosophy and Kether-Chochmah-Binah in the Zohar. The First Manifested Logos is the Potentia, the unrevealed Cause; the Second, the still latent Thought; the Third, the Demiurgus, the active Will evolving from its universal Self the active effect, which, in its turn, becomes the cause on a lower plane.

Q. What is Ever-Darkness in the sense used here?

A. Ever-Darkness means, I suppose, the ever-unknowable mystery, behind the veil—in fact, Parabrahm. Even the Logos can see only Mulaprakriti, it cannot see that which is beyond the veil. It is that which is the "Ever-unknowable Darkness".

Q. What is the Ray in this connection?

A. I will recapitulate. We have the plane of the circle, the face being black, the point in the circle being potentially white, and this is the first possible conception in our minds of the invisible Logos. "Ever-Darkness" is eternal, the Ray periodical. Having flashed out from this central point and thrilled through the Germ, the Ray is withdrawn again within this point and the Germ developes into the Second Logos, the triangle within the Mundane Egg.

Q. *What, then, are the stages of manifestation?*

A. The first stage is the appearance of the potential point in the circle—the unmanifested Logos. The second stage is the shooting forth of the Ray from the potential white point, producing the first point, which is called, in the Zohar, Kether or Sephira. The third stage is the production from Kether of Chochmah, and Binah, thus constituting the first triangle, which is the Third or manifested Logos—in other words, the subjective and objective Universe. Further, from this manifested Logos will proceed the Seven Rays, which in the Zohar are called the lower Sephiroth and in Eastern occultism the primordial seven rays. Thence will proceed the innumerable series of Hierarchies.

Q. *Is the Triangle here mentioned that which you refer to as the Germ in the Mundane Egg?*

A. Certainly it is. But you must remember that there are both the Universal and Solar Eggs (as well as others), and that it is necessary to qualify any statement made concerning them. The Mundane Egg is an expression of Abstract Form.

Q. *May Abstract Form be called the first manifestation of the eternal female principle?*

A. It is the first manifestation not of the female principle, but of the Ray which proceeds from the central point which is perfectly sexless. There is no eternal female principle, for this Ray produces that which is the united potentiality of both sexes but is by no means either male or female. This latter differentiation will only appear when it falls into matter, when the Triangle becomes a Square, the first Tetraktys.

Q. *Then the Mundane Egg is as sexless as the Ray?*

A. The Mundane Egg is simply the first stage of manifestation, undifferentiated primordial matter, in which the vital creative Germ receives its first spiritual impulse; Potentiality becomes Potency.

Matter, by convenience of metaphor, only, is regarded as feminine, because it is receptive of the rays of the sun which fecundate it and so produce all that grows on its surface, *i.e.*, on this the lowest plane. On the other hand primordial matter should be regarded as substance, and by no means can be spoken of as having sex.

Thus the Egg, on whatever plane you speak of, means the ever-existing undifferentiated matter which strictly is not matter at all but, as we call it, the Atoms. Matter is destructible in form while the Atoms are absolutely indestructible, being the quintessence of Substances. And here, I mean by " atoms " the primordial divine Units, not the " atoms " of modern Science.

Similarly the " Germ " is a figurative expression; the germ is everywhere, even as the circle whose circumference is nowhere and whose centre is everywhere. It therefore means all germs, that is to say, unmanifested nature, or the whole creative power which will emanate, called by the Hindus Brahmâ, though on every plane it has a different name.

Q. *Is the Matri-Padma the eternal or the periodical Egg ?*

A. The eternal Egg; it will become periodical only when the ray from the first Logos shall have flashed from the latent Germ in the Matri-Padma which is the Egg, the Womb of the Universe which is to be. By analogy, the physical germ in the female cell could not be called eternal, though the latent spirit of the germ concealed within the male cell in nature, may be so called.

Sloka (4). HER HEART HAD NOT YET OPENED FOR THE ONE RAY TO ENTER, THENCE TO FALL AS THREE INTO FOUR IN THE LAP OF MAYA.

" But as the hour strikes and it becomes receptive of the Fohatic impress of the Divine Thought (the Logos or the male aspect of the Anima Mundi, Alaya)—its heart opens."*

Q. *Does not the Fohatic impress of the Divine Thought apply to a later stage of differentiation ?*

A. Fohat, as a distinct force or entity, is a later development. "Fohatic " is an adjective and may be used in a more wide sense; Fohat, as a substantive, or Entity, springs from a Fohatic attribute of the Logos. Electricity cannot be generated from that which does not contain an electric principle or element. The divine principle is eternal, the gods are periodical. Fohat is the Sakti or force of the divine mind; Brahmâ and Fohat are both aspects of the divine mind.

Q. *Is it not the intention in the Commentaries to this Stanza to convey some idea of the subject by speaking of correspondences in a much later stage of evolution ?*

A. Exactly so; it has several times been stated that the Commentaries on the First Volume are almost entirely concerned with the evolution of the solar system only. The beauty and wisdom of the Stanzas consist in this, that they may be interpreted on seven different planes, the last

---

* Vol. I. p. 58.

reflecting, by the universal law of correspondences and analogy, in its most differentiated, gross and physical aspect, the process which takes place on the first or purely spiritual plane. I may state here once for all that the first Stanzas treat of the awakening from Pralaya and are not concerned with the Solar system alone, while Vol. II. deals only with our Earth.

Q. Can you say what is the real meaning of the word Fohat?

A. The word is a Turanian compound and its meanings are various. In China *Pho*, or *Fo*, is the word for " animal soul ", the vital *Nephesh* or the breath of life. Some say that it is derived from the Sanscrit " Bhu ", meaning existence, or rather the essence of existence. Now Swayambhu means Brahmâ and Man at the same time. It means self-existence and self-existing, that which is everlasting, the eternal breath. If Sat is the potentiality of Being, Pho is the potency of Being. The meaning, however, entirely depends upon the position of the accent. Again, Fohat is related to Mahat. It is the reflection of the Universal Mind, the synthesis of the " Seven " and the intelligences of the seven creative Builders, or, as we call them, Cosmocratores. Hence, as you will understand, life and electricity are one in our philosophy. They say life is electricity, and if so, then the One Life is the essence and root of all the electric and magnetic phenomena on this manifested plane.

Q. How is it that Horus and the other " Son-Gods " are said to be born " through an immaculate Mother " ?

A. On the first plane of differentiation there is no sex—to use the term for convenience' sake—but both sexes exist potentially in primordial matter. Matter is the root of the word " mother " and therefore female; but there are two kinds of matter. The undifferentiated, primordial matter is not fecundated by some act in space and time, fertility and productiveness being inherent in it. Therefore that which emanates or is *born* out of that inherent virtue is not born from, but through, it. In other words, that virtue or quality is the sole cause that this something manifests through its vehicle; whereas on the physical plane, Mother-matter is not the active cause but the passive means and instrument of an independent cause.

In the Christian doctrine of the Immaculate Conception—a materializing of the metaphysical and spiritual conception—the mother is first fecundated by the Holy Ghost and the Child born from, and not through, her. " From " implies that there is a limited and conditioned source to start from, the act having to take place in Space and Time. " Through " is applicable to Eternity and Infinity as well as to the Finite. The Great Breath thrills through Space, which is boundless, and is *in*, not *from*, eternity.

Q. How does the Triangle become the Square, and the Square the six-faced Cube?

A. In occult and Pythagorean geometry the Tetrad is said to combine within itself all the materials from which Kosmos is produced. The Point or One, extends to a Line—the Two; a Line to a Superficies, Three; and the Superficies, Triad or Triangle, is converted into a Solid, the Tetrad or Four, by the point being placed over it. Kabalistically Kether, or Sephira, the Point, emanates Chochmah and Binah, which two, are the synonym of *Mahat*, in the Hindu Purânas, and this Triad, descending into matter, produces the Tetragrammaton, *Tetraktys*, as also the lower Tetrad. This number contains both the productive and produced numbers. The Duad doubled makes a Tetrad and the Tetrad doubled forms a Hebdomad. From another point of view it is the Spirit, Will, and Intellect animating the four lower principles.

Q. Then how does the Square become the six-faced Cube?

A. The Square becomes the Cube when each point of the triangle becomes dual, male or female. The Pythagoreans said " Once One, Twice Two, and there ariseth a Tetrad, having on its top the highest Unit; it becomes a Pyramid whose base is a plane Tetrad; divine light resting on it, makes the abstract Cube ".

The surface of the Cube is composed of six squares, and the Cube unfolded gives the Cross, or the vertical Four, barred by the horizontal Three; the six thus making Seven, the seven principles or the Pythagorean seven properties in man. See the excellent explanation given of this in Mr. R. Skinner's *Source of Measures*.

" Thus is repeated on earth the mystery enacted, according to the Seers, on the divine plane. The ' Son ' of the immaculate Celestial Virgin (or the undifferentiated cosmic protyle—Matter in its infinitude) is born again on Earth as the son of the terrestrial Eve—our mother Earth, and becomes Humanity as a total—past, present and future—for Jehovah or Jod-He-Vau-He is androgyne, or both male and female. Above, the ' Son ' is the whole Kosmos; below, he is Mankind. The Triad or Triangle becomes the Tetraktys, the sacred Pythagorean number, the perfect Square and six-faced Cube on Earth. The Macroprosopus (the Great Face) is now Microprosopus (The Lesser Face); or, as the Kabalists have it, the ' Ancient of Days' descending on Adam Kadmon whom he uses as his vehicle to manifest through, gets transformed into Tetragrammaton. It is now in the lap of Maya, the Great Illusion, and between itself and the Reality has the Astral Light, the great deceiver of man's limited senses, unless Knowledge through Paramarthasatya comes to the rescue."*

---

* Vol. I. p. 60.

That is to say, the Logos becomes a Tetragrammaton; the Triangle, or the Three becomes the Four.

Q. Is the Astral Light used here in the sense of Maya ?

A. Certainly. It is explained further on in the *Secret Doctrine* that practically there are only four planes belonging to the planetary chains. The three higher planes are absolutely *Arupa* and outside our comprehension.

Q. Then the Tetraktys is entirely different from Tetragrammaton ?

A. The Tetraktys by which the Pythagoreans swore, was not the Tetragrammaton, but on the contrary, the higher or superior Tetraktys. In the opening chapters of *Genesis* we have a clue to the discovery of this lower Tetragrammaton. We there find Adam, Eve, and Jehovah who becomes Cain. The further extension of Humanity is symbolised in Abel, as the human conception of the higher. Abel is the daughter and not the son of Eve, and symbolises the separation of the sexes; while the murder of Abel is symbolical of marriage. The still more human conception is found at the end of the fourth Chapter, when speaking of Seth, to whom was born a son Enos, after which men began—not, as translated in Genesis, to "call upon the Lord"—but to be called *Jod-He-Vah*, meaning males and females.

The Tetragrammaton, therefore, is simply Malkuth; when the bridegroom comes to the bride on Earth, then it becomes Humanity. The seven lower Sephiroth must all be passed through, the Tetragrammaton becoming more and more material. The Astral Plane lies between the *Tetraktys* and Tetragrammaton.

Q. Tetraktys appears to be used here in two entirely different senses ?

The true Pythagorean Tetraktys was the Tetraktys of the invisible Monad, which produces the first Point, the second and the third and then retires into the darkness and everlasting silence; in other words the Tetraktys is the first Logos. Taken from the plane of matter, it is among other things, the lower Quaternary, the man of flesh or matter.

VI.

*Meeting held at 17, Lansdowne Road, London, W., on February 14th, 1889;
Mr. W. KINGSLAND in the chair.*

STANZA III.

Sloka (1). THE LAST VIBRATION OF THE SEVENTH ETERNITY THRILLS THROUGH INFINITUDE. THE MOTHER SWELLS, EXPANDING FROM WITHIN WITHOUT LIKE THE BUD OF THE LOTUS.

" The seemingly paradoxical use of the sentence ' Seventh Eternity ', thus dividing the invisible, is sanctified in esoteric philosophy. The latter divides boundless duration into unconditionally eternal and universal time, and a conditioned one (Khandakâla). One is the abstraction or noumenon of infinite Time (Kâla) the other its phenomenon appearing periodically as the effect of MAHAT (the universal Intelligence limited by Manvantaric duration)."*

Q. Does the commencement of Time as distinguished from Duration, correspond to the appearance of the manifested Logos?

A. Certainly it cannot do so earlier. But "the seventh vibration" applies to both the First, and to the manifested Logos—the first out of Space and Time, the second, when Time has commenced. It is only when "the mother swells" that differentiation sets in, for when the first Logos radiates through primordial and undifferentiated matter there is as yet no action in Chaos. "The last vibration of the Seventh Eternity" is the first which announces the Dawn, and is a synonym for the First or unmanifested Logos. There is no Time at this stage. There is neither Space nor Time when beginning is made; but it is all in space and Time, once that differentiation sets in. At the time of the primordial radiation, or when the Second Logos emanates, it is Father-Mother potentially, but when the Third or manifested Logos appears, it becomes the Virgin-Mother. The "Father and the Son" are one in all the world Theogonies; hence, the expression corresponds to the appearance of both the unmanifested and the manifested Logos, one at the beginning, the other at the end, of the "Seventh Eternity".

---

* Vol. I. p. 62.

Q. Can you, then, speak of Time as existing from the appearance of the Second or Unmanifested-Manifested Logos?

A. Assuredly not, but from the appearance of the Third. It is here that the great difference between the two lies, as just shown. The "last vibration" begins outside of Time and Space, and ends with the third Logos, when Time and Space begin, *i.e.*, periodical time. The Second Logos partaking of both the essences or natures of the first and the last. There is no differentiation with the First Logos; differentiation only begins in latent World-Thought, with the Second Logos, and receives its full expression, *i.e.*, becomes the "Word" made flesh—with the Third.

Q. How do the terms "Radiation" and "Emanation" differ in the Secret Doctrine?

A. They express, to my mind, two entirely different ideas, and are the best apologies for the original terms that could be found; but if the ordinary meanings are attached to them the idea will be missed. Radiation is, so to say, the unconscious and spontaneous shooting forth, the action of a something from which this act takes place; but emanation is something from which another thing issues in a constant efflux, and emanates consciously. An orthodox Occultist goes so far as to say that the smell of a flower emanates from it "consciously"—absurd as it may seem to the profane. Radiation *can* come from the Absolute; Emanation *cannot*. One difference exists in the idea that Radiation is sure, sooner or later, to be withdrawn again while Emanation runs into other emanations and is thoroughly separated and differentiated. Of course at the end of the cycle of time emanation will also be withdrawn into the One Absolute; but meanwhile, during the entire cycle of changes emanation will persist. One thing emanates from the other, and, in fact, from one point of view, emanation is equivalent to Evolution; while "radiation" represents to my mind—in the precosmic period, of course—an instantaneous action like that of a piece of paper set on fire under a burning glass, of which act the Sun knows nothing. Both terms, of course, are used for want of better.

Q. What is meant by prototypes existing in the Astral Light?*

A. Astral Light is here used as a convenient phrase for a term very little understood, viz: "the realm of Akâsa, or primordial Light manifested through the divine Ideation". The latter must be accepted in this particular case as a generic term for the universal and divine mind reflected in the waters of Space or Chaos, which is the Astral Light proper, and a mirror reflecting and reversing a higher plane. In the

---

* Vol. I. p. 63.

ABSOLUTE or Divine Thought everything exists and there has been no time when it did not so exist; but Divine Ideation is limited by the Universal Manvantaras. The realm of Akâsa is the undifferentiated noumenal and abstract Space which will be occupied by *Chidakasam*, the field of primordial consciousness. It has several degrees, however, in Occult philosophy; in fact, " seven fields ". The first is the field of latent consciousness which is coeval with the duration of the first and second unmanifested Logoi. It is the " Light which shineth in darkness and the darkness comprehended it not " of St. John's Gospel. When the hour strikes for the Third Logos to appear, then from the latent potentiality there radiates a lower field of differentiated consciousness, which is Mahat, or the entire collectivity of those Dhyan Chohans of *sentient life* of which Fohat is the representative on the objective plane and the Manasa-putras on the subjective. The Astral Light is that which mirrors the three higher planes of consciousness, and is above the lower, or terrestrial plane; therefore it does not extend beyond the fourth plane, where, one may say, the Akâsa begins.

There is one great difference between the Astral Light and the Akâsa which must be remembered. The latter is eternal, the former is periodic. The Astral Light changes not only with the Mahamanvantaras but also with every sub-period and planetary cycle or Round.

Q. Then do the prototypes exist on a plane higher than that of the Astral Light ?

A. The prototypes or ideas of things exist first on the plane of Divine eternal Consciousness and thence become reflected and reversed in the Astral Light, which also reflects on its lower individual plane the life of our Earth, recording it on its " tablets ". Therefore, is the Astral Light called illusion. It is from this that we, in our turn, get our prototypes. Consequently unless the Clairvoyant or SEER can get beyond this plane of illusion, he can never see the Truth, but will be drowned in an ocean of self-deception and hallucinations.

Q. And what is the Akâsa proper ?

A. The Akâsa is the eternal divine consciousness which cannot differentiate, have qualities, or act; action belongs to that which is reflected or mirrored from it. The unconditioned and infinite can have no relation with the finite and conditioned. The Astral Light is the Middle Heaven of the Gnostics, in which is Sophia Achamoth, the mother of the seven builders or Spirits of the Earth, which are not necessarily good, and among which the Gnostics placed Jehovah, whom they called Ildabaoth. *(Sophia Achamoth must not be confounded with the divine Sophia.)* We may compare the Akâsa and the Astral Light, with regard to these prototypes, to the germ in the acorn. The latter, besides containing in itself the astral form of the future oak, conceals the germ from which grows a tree containing millions of forms. These forms are contained in the acorn potentially, yet the development of each particular acorn depends upon extraneous circumstances, physical forces, &c.

Q. But how does this account for the endless varieties of the Vegetable Kingdom ?

A. The different variations of plants, &c., are the broken rays of one Ray. As the ray passes through the seven planes, it is broken on every plane into thousands and millions of rays down to the world of forms, every ray breaking into an intelligence on its own plane. So that we see every plant has an intelligence, or its own purpose of life, so to speak, and its own freewill, to a degree. This is how, I, at any rate, understand it. A plant can be receptive or non-receptive, though *every plant without an exception* feels and has a consciousness of its own. But besides the latter, every plant—from the gigantic tree down to the minutest fern or blade of grass—has, Occultism teaches us, an Elemental entity of which it is the outward clothing on this plane. Hence, the Kabalists and the mediæval Rosicrucians are always found talking of Elementals. According to them, everything possessed an Elemental sprite.

Q. What is the difference between an Elemental and a Dhyan Chohan or Dhyani Buddha ?

A. The difference is very great. Elementals are attached only to the four terrestrial Elements and only to the two lower kingdoms of nature— the mineral and the vegetable—in which they *inmetalize* and *inherbalize*, so to speak. The Hindu term *Deva* may be applied to them, but not that of *Dhyan Chohan*. The former have a kind of Kosmic intelligence; but the latter are endowed with a supersensuous intellect, each of its kind. As to the Dhyani Buddhas, they belong to the highest Divine (or omniscient) Intelligences, answering best, perhaps, to the Roman Catholic Archangels.

Q. Is there an evolution of types through the various planes of the Astral Light ?

A. You must follow out the simile of the evolution of the acorn. From the acorn will grow an oak and this oak, as a tree, may have a thousand forms, all of which vary the one from the other. All these forms are contained within the acorn, and though the form which the tree will take depends on extraneous circumstances, yet that, which Aristotle called the " privation of matter " exists beforehand, in the Astral waves. But the noumenal germ of the oak exists beyond the plane of the Astral Light ; it is only the subjective picture of it that already exists in the Astral Light, and the development of the oak tree is the result of the developed prototype in the Astral Light, which development proceeds from higher to lower planes, until on the lowest plane it has its last consolidation and development of form. And here is the explanation of the curious fact according to the Vedantin assertion that each plant has its Karma and that its growth is the result of Karma. This Karma proceeds from the lower Dhyan Chohans who trace out and plan the growth of the tree.

Q. What is the real meaning of Manvantara or rather Manu-antara ?

A. It means really " Between two Manus ", of which there are fourteen in every " Day of Brahmâ ", such a " Day " consisting of 1,000 aggregates of four ages or 1,000 " Great Ages ", Mahayugas. When the word " Manu " is analysed it is found that Orientalists state that it is from the root " Man " to think, hence the thinking man. But, esoterically every Manu, as an anthropomorphized patron of his special cycle, or Round, is but the personified idea of the " Thought Divine " (like the Hermetic Pymander). Each of the Manus, therefore, is the special god, the creator and fashioner of all that appears during his own respective cycle of being or Manvantara.

Q. Is Manu a unity also of human consciousness personified, or is it the individualization of the Thought Divine for manvantaric purposes ?

A. Of both, since " human consciousness " is but a Ray of the Divine. Our *Manas*, or Ego, proceeds from, and is the Son (figuratively) of Mahat. Vaivasvata Manu (the Manu of our own fifth race and Humanity in general) is the chief personified representative of the *thinking* Humanity of the fifth Root-race; and therefore he is represented as the eldest Son of the Sun and an *Agnishwatta* Ancestor. As " *Manu* " is derived from *Man*, to think, the idea is clear. Thought in its action on human brains is endless. Thus Manu is, and contains the potentiality of all the thinking forms which will be developed on earth from this particular source. In the exoteric teaching he is the beginning of this earth, and from him and his daughter Ila humanity is born; he is a unity which contains all the pluralities and their modifications. Every Manvantara has thus its own Manu and from this Manu the various Manus or rather all the *Manasa* of the Kalpas will proceed. As an analogy he may be compared to the white light which contains all the other rays, giving birth to them by passing through the prism of differentiation and evolution. But this pertains to the esoteric and metaphysical teachings.

Q. Is it possible to say that Manu stands in relation to each Manvantara as does the First Logos to the Mahamanvantara ?

A. It is possible to say so, if you like.

Q. Is it possible to say that Manu is an individuality ?

A. In the abstract sense certainly not, but it is possible to apply an analogy. Manu is the synthesis perhaps of the Manasa, and he is a single consciousness in the same sense that while all the different cells of which the human body is composed are different and varying consciousnesses there is still a unit of consciousness which is the man. But this unit, so to say, is not a single consciousness: it is a reflection of thousands and millions of consciousnesses which a man has absorbed.

But Manu is not really an individuality, it is the whole of mankind. You may say that Manu is a generic name for the Pitris, the progenitors of mankind. They come, as I have shown, from the Lunar Chain. They give birth to humanity, for, having become the first men, they give birth to others by evolving their shadows, their astral selves. They not only give birth to humanity but to animals and all other creatures. In this sense it is said in the Purânas of the great Yogis that they gave birth, one to all the serpents, another to all the birds, &c. But, as the moon receives its light from the Sun, so the descendants of the Lunar Pitris receive their higher mental light from the Sun or the " Son of the Sun ". For all you know Vaivasvata Manu may be an *Avatar* or a personification of MAHAT, commissioned by the Universal Mind to lead and guide thinking Humanity onwards.

Q. We learn that the perfected humanity of one Round becomes the Dhyani-Buddhas and the guiding rulers of the next Manvantara. What bearing then has Manu on the hosts of the Dhyani-Buddhas ?

A. He has no bearing at all—in exoteric teachings. But I may tell you that the Dhyani-Buddhas have nothing to do with the lower practical work of the earth-plane. To use an illustration: the Dhyani-Buddha may be compared to a great ruler of any condition of life. Suppose that it were merely that of a house: the great ruler has nothing directly to do with the dirty work of a kitchen-maid. The higher Dhyanis evolve lower and lower hierarchies of Dhyanis more and more consolidated and more material until we arrive at this chain of Planets, some of the latter being the Manus, Pitris and Lunar Ancestors. As I show in the Second Volume of the *Secret Doctrine*, these Pitris have the task of giving birth to man. They do this by projecting their shadows and the first humanity (if indeed it can be called humanity) are the astral Chhayas of the Lunar Ancestors over which physical nature builds the physical body, which at first is formless. The Second Race is more and more formed and is sexless. In the Third Race they become bi-sexual and hermaphrodite and then finally separating, the propagation of humanity proceeds in diverse manners.

Q. Then what do you mean by the term Manvantara, or as you have explained it Manu-antara, or " between two Manus " ?

A. It simply means a period of activity and is not used in any limited and definite sense. You have to gather from the context of the work you are studying what the meaning of the Manvantara is, remembering also that what is applicable to a lesser period applies also to a greater, and conversely.

Q. Is " Water " as used here purely symbolical or has it a correspondence in the evolution of the elements ?*

A. It is necessary to be very careful not to confuse the universal with the terrestrial elements. Nor again do the terrestrial elements mean what is known as the chemical elements. I would call the cosmic, universal elements the noumena of the terrestrial elements, and add that cosmic is not confined to our little Solar System.

Water is the first cosmic element and the terms " darkness " and " chaos " are used to denote the same " element ". There are seven states of matter of which three are generally known, viz., solid, liquid, and gaseous. It is necessary to consider everything cosmic and terrestrial as existing in variations of these seven states. But it is impossible for me to speak in terms which are unknown to you, and therefore impossible to understand. Thus " water ", the " hot and moyst principle " of the philosophers, is used to denote that which is not yet solid matter, or rather that which does not yet possess the solidity of matter, as we understand it. It is rendered rather more difficult by the use of the term " water " as a subsequent " element " in the series of ether, fire and air. But ether contains in itself all the others and their properties, and it is this ether which is the hypothetical agent of physical science: moreover it is the lowest form of Akâsa, the one agent and universal element. Thus water is used here to denote matter in its precosmic state.

Q. What relation have the elements to the Elementals ?

A. The same relation as the earth has to man. As physical man is the quintessence of the Earth, so Air or Fire, or Water, an Elemental (called Sylph, Salamander, Undine, etc.,) is of the quintessence of its special element. Every differentiation of substance and matter, evolves a kind of intelligent Force, and it is these which the Rosicrucians called Elemental or Nature spirits. Everyone of us can believe in Elementals which we can create for ourselves. But this latter class of elemental creation has no existence outside our own imagination. It will be an intelligence, a Force, good or bad, but the form given to it and its attributes will be of our own creation, while at the same time it will have an intelligence derived also from us.

Q. Are the " Virgin-Egg " and the " Eternal Egg " the same thing, or are they different stages of differentiation ?

---

* Vol. I. p. 64.

A. The eternal egg is a pre-differentiation in a laya or zero condition; thus, before differentiation it can have neither attributes nor qualities. The "virgin egg" is already qualified and therefore differentiated, although in its essence it is the same. No one thing can be separated from another thing, in its abstract essential nature. But in the world of illusion, in the world of forms, of differentiation, everything, ourselves included, *seems* to be so separated.

VII.

Meeting held at 17, Lansdowne Road, London, W., on February 21st, 1889; Mr. W. Kingsland in the chair.

STANZA III. (*continued*).

Sloka (2). THE VIBRATION SWEEPS ALONG, TOUCHING WITH ITS SWIFT WING (*simultaneously*) THE WHOLE UNIVERSE; AND THE GERM THAT DWELLETH IN DARKNESS: THE DARKNESS THAT BREATHES (*moves*) OVER THE SLUMBERING WATERS OF LIFE.

Q. How are we to understand the expression that the vibration touches the whole universe and also the germ?

A. First of all the terms used must be defined as far as possible, for the language used is purely figurative. The Universe does not mean the Kosmos or world of forms but the formless space, the future vehicle of the Universe which will be manifested. This space is synonymous with the "waters of space", with (to us) eternal darkness, in fact with Parabrahm. In short the whole Sloka refers to the "period" before there was any manifestation whatever. In the same way the Germ—the Germ is eternal, the undifferentiated atoms of future matter—is one with space, as infinite as it is indestructible, and as eternal as space itself. Similarly with "vibration", which corresponds with the Point, the unmanifested Logos.

It is necessary to add one important explanation. In using figurative language, as has been done in the *Secret Doctrine*, analogies and comparisons are very frequent. Darkness for instance, as a rule, applies only to the unknown totality, or, Absoluteness. Contrasted with eternal darkness the first Logos is certainly, Light; contrasted with the second or third, the manifested Logoi, the first is Darkness, and the others are Light.

Sloka (3). DARKNESS RADIATES LIGHT, AND LIGHT DROPS ONE SOLITARY RAY INTO THE WATERS, THE MOTHER-DEEP. THE RAY SHOOTS THROUGH THE VIRGIN EGG; THE RAY CAUSES THE ETERNAL EGG TO THRILL, AND DROP THE NON-ETERNAL (*periodical*) GERM, WHICH CONDENSES INTO THE WORLD-EGG.

Q. Why is Light said to drop one solitary ray into the waters and how is this ray represented in connection with the Triangle?

A. However many the Rays may appear to be on this plane, when brought back to their original source they will finally be resolved into a unity, like the seven prismatic colours which all proceed from, and are resolved into the one white ray. Thus too, this one solitary Ray expands into the seven rays (and their innumerable sub-divisions) on the plane of illusion only. It is represented in connection with the Triangle because the Triangle is the first perfect geometrical figure. As stated by Pythagoras, and also in the Stanza, the Ray (the Pythagorean Monad) descending from " no-place " (*Aloka*), shoots like a falling star through the planes of non-being into the first world of being, and gives birth to Number One; then branching off, to the right, it produces Number Two; turning again to form the base-line it begets Number Three, and thence ascending again to Number One, it finally disappears therefrom into the realms of non-being as Pythagoras shows.

Q. Why should Pythagorean teachings be found in old Hindu philosophies?

A. Pythagoras derived this teaching from India and in the old books we find him spoken of as the Yavanacharya or Greek Teacher. Thus we see that the Triangle is the first differentiation, its sides however all being described by the one Ray.

Q. What is really meant by the term " planes of non-being ".

A. In using the term " planes of non-being " it is necessary to remember that these planes are only to us spheres of non-being, but those of being and matter to higher intelligences than ourselves. The highest Dhyan-Chohans of the Solar System can have no conception of that which exists in higher systems, *i.e.*, on the second " septenary " Kosmic plane, which to the Beings of the ever *invisible* Universe is entirely subjective.

Sloka (4). (*Then*) THE THREE (*Triangle*) FALL INTO THE FOUR (*Quaternary*). THE RADIANT ESSENCE BECOMES SEVEN INSIDE, SEVEN OUTSIDE. THE LUMINOUS EGG (*Hiranyagharba*), WHICH IN ITSELF IS THREE (*the triple hypostases of Brahma, or Vishnu, the three Avasthas*) CURDLES AND SPREADS IN MILKWHITE CURDS THROUGHOUT THE DEPTHS OF MOTHER, THE ROOT THAT GROWS IN THE OCEAN OF LIFE.

Q. Is the Radiant Essence the same as the luminous Egg? What is the Root that grows in the ocean of life?

A. The radiant essence, luminous egg or Golden Egg of Brahmâ, or again, Hiranyagharba, are identical. The Root that grows in the ocean of life is the potentiality that transforms into objective differentiated matter the universal, subjective, ubiquitous but homogeneous germ, or the eternal essence which contains the potency of abstract nature. The Ocean of Life is, according to a term of the Vedanta philosophy—if I mistake not—the " One Life", Paramatma, when the transcendental supreme Soul is meant; and Jivatma, when we speak of the physical and animal " breath of life " or, so to speak, the differentiated soul, that life in short, which gives being to the atom and the universe, the molecule and the man, the animal, plant, and mineral.

" The Radiant Essence curdled and spread through the depths of Space." From an astronomical point of view this is easy of explanation: it is the Milky Way, the world-stuff, or primordial matter in its first form.

Q. Is the Radiant Essence, Milky Way, or world-stuff, resolvable into atoms, or is it non-atomic?

A. In its precosmic state it is of course, non-atomic, if by atoms you mean molecules; for the hypothetical atom, a mere mathematical point, is not material or application to matter, nor even to substance. The real atom does not exist on the material plane. The definition of a point as having position, must not, in Occultism, be taken in the ordinary sense of location; as the *real* atom is beyond space and time. The word molecular is really applicable to our globe and its plane, only: once inside of it, even on the other globes of our planetary chain, matter is in quite another condition, and non-molecular. The atom is in its eternal state, invisible even to the eye of an Archangel; and becomes visible to the latter only periodically, during the life cycle. The particle, or molecule, *is not*, but exists periodically, and is therefore regarded as an illusion.

The world-stuff informs itself through various planes and cannot be said to be resolved into stars or to have become molecular until it reaches the plane of being of the visible or objective Universe.

Q. Can ether be said to be molecular in Occultism?

A. It entirely depends upon what is meant by the term. In its lowest strata, where it merges with the astral light, it may be called molecular on its own plane; but not for us. But the ether of which science has a suspicion, is the grossest manifestation of Akâsa, though on our plane, for us mortals, it is the seventh principle of the astral light, and three degrees higher than " radiant matter". When it penetrates, or informs something, it may be molecular because it takes on the form of the latter, and its atoms inform the particles of that " something". We may perhaps call matter " crystallised ether ".

Q. But what is an atom, in fact?

A. An atom may be compared to (and is for the Occultist) the seventh principle of a body or rather of a molecule. The physical or chemical molecule is composed of an infinity of finer molecules and these in their turn of innumerable and still finer molecules. Take for instance a molecule of iron and so resolve it that it becomes non-molecular; it is then, at once transformed into one of its seven principles, *viz.*, its astral body; the seventh of these is the atom. The analogy between a molecule of iron, before it is broken up, and this same molecule after resolution, is the same as that between a physical body before and after death. The principles remain *minus* the body. Of course this is occult alchemy, not modern chemistry.

Q. What is the meaning of the allegorical " churning of the ocean", and " cow of plenty " of the Hindus, and what correspondence is there between them and the " war in heaven "?

A. A process which begins in the state of "non-being," and ends with the close of Maha-Pralaya, can hardly be given in a few words or even volumes. It is simply an allegorical representation of the unseen and unknown primeval intelligences, the atoms of occult science, Brahmâ himself being called *Anu* or the Atom, fashioning and differentiating the shoreless ocean of the primordial radiant essence. The relation and correspondence between the "churning of the ocean" and the "war in heaven" is a very long and abtruse subject to handle. To give it in its lowest symbolical aspect, this "war in heaven" is going on eternally. Differentiation is contrast, the equilibrium of contraries: and so long as this exists there will be "war" or fighting. There are, of course, different stages and aspects of this war: such for instance as the astronomical and physical. For everyone and everything that is born in a Manvantara, there is "war in heaven" and also on the earth: for the fourteen Root and Seed-Manus who preside over our Manvantaric cycle, and for the countless *Forces*, human or otherwise, that proceed from them. There is a perpetual struggle of adjustment, for everything tends to harmonise and equilibrate; in fact it must do so before it can assume any shape. The elements of which we are formed, the particles of our bodies, are in a continual war, one crowding out the other and changing with every moment. At the "Churning of the Ocean" by the gods, the Nagas came and some stole of the Amrita—the water of Immortality,—and thence arose war between the gods and the Asuras, the *no*-gods, and the gods were worsted. This refers to the formation of the Universe and the differentiation of the primordial primeval matter. But you must remember, that this is only the cosmogonical aspect,—one out of the seven meanings. The war in heaven had also immediate reference to the evolution of the intellectual principle in mankind. This is the metaphysical key.

Q. Why are numbers so much used in the Stanzas; and what is really the secret of their being so freely used in the World-Scriptures—in the Bible and in the Purânas, by Pythagoras and by the Aryan Sages?

A. Balzac, the unconscious occultist of French literature, says somewhere, "the Number is to Mind the same as it is to matter, an incomprehensible agent. But I would answer—perhaps so to the profane, never to the initiated mind. Number is, as the great writer thought, an Entity, and at the same time, a Breath emanating from what he called God and what we call the ALL; the breath which alone could organise the physical Kosmos, 'where nought obtains its form but through the Deity, which is an effort of Number.'"* "God geometrizes" says Plato.

Q. In what sense can numbers be called Entities?

A. When intelligent Entities are meant; when they are regarded simply as digits they are, of course, not Entities but symbolical signs.

Q. Why is the radiant essence said to become seven inside and seven outside?

A. Because it has seven principles on the plane of the manifested and seven on that of the unmanifested. Always argue on analogy and apply the old occult axiom "As above so below".

Q. But are the planes of "non-being" also Septenary?

A. Most undeniably. That which in the *Secret Doctrine* is referred to as the unmanifested planes, are unmanifested or planes of non-being only from the point of view of the finite intellect; to higher intelligences they would be manifested planes and so on to infinity, analogy always holding good.

---

* Vol. i., p. 66.

VIII.

Meeting held at 17, Lansdowne Road, London, W., on February 28th, 1889; Mr. W. Kingsland in the chair.

STANZA III. (*continued*).

THE ROOT REMAINS, THE LIGHT REMAINS, THE CURDS REMAIN, AND STILL OEAOHOO IS ONE.

Q. What is meant by saying that these remain ?

A. It means simply that whatever the plurality of manifestation may be, still it is all one. In other words these are all different aspects of the one element; it does not mean that they remain without differentiation.

"The curds are the first differentiation and probably refer to that cosmic matter which is supposed to be the origin of the ' Milky Way '—the matter we know. This 'matter', which, according to the revelation received from the primeval Dhyani-Buddhas, is, during the periodical sleep of the universe, of the ultimate tenuity conceivable to the eye of the perfect Bodhisatva—this matter, radiant and cool, becomes at the first re-awakening of cosmic motion, scattered through space, appearing when seen from the earth, in clusters and lumps, like curds in thin milk. These are the seeds of future worlds, the ' star-stuff '."*

Q. Is it to be supposed that the Milky Way is composed of matter in a state of differentiation other than that with which we are acquainted ?

A. I thoroughly believe so. It is the store-house of the materials from which the stars, planets and other celestial bodies are produced. Matter in this state does not exist on earth; but that which is already differentiated and found on earth is also found on other planets and *vice-versâ*. But, as I understand, before reaching the planets from its condition in the Milky Way matter has first to pass through many stages of differentiation. The matter, for instance, within the Solar system is in an entirely different state from that which is outside or beyond the system.

Q. Is there a difference between the Nebulae and the Milky Way ?

A. The same, I should say, that there is between a highway road and the stones and mud upon that road. There must be, of course, a differ-

---

* Vol. i., p. 69.

ence between the matter of the Milky Way and that of the various Nebulæ, and these again must differ among themselves. But in all your scientific calculations and measurements it is necessary to consider that the light by which the objects are seen is a *reflected* light, and the optical illusion caused by the atmosphere of the earth renders it impossible that calculations of distances, &c., should be absolutely correct, in addition to the fact that it entirely alters observations of the matter of which the celestial bodies are composed, as it is liable to impose upon us a constitution similar to that of the earth. This is, at any rate, what the MASTERS teach us.

Sloka (6). THE ROOT OF LIFE WAS IN EVERY DROP OF THE OCEAN OF IMMORTALITY *(Amrita)* AND THE OCEAN WAS RADIANT LIGHT, WHICH WAS FIRE AND HEAT AND MOTION. DARKNESS VANISHED AND WAS NO MORE. IT DISAPPEARED IN ITS OWN ESSENCE, THE BODY OF FIRE AND WATER, OF FATHER AND MOTHER.

Q. What are the various meanings of the term "fire" on the different planes of Kosmos?

A. Fire is the most mystic of all the five elements, as also the most divine. Therefore to give an explanation of its various meanings on our plane alone, leaving all the other planes entirely out of the question, would be much too arduous, in addition to its being entirely incomprehensible for the vast majority. Fire is the father of light, light the parent of heat and air (vital air). If the absolute deity can be referred to as Darkness or the Dark Fire, the light, its first progeny, is truly the first self-conscious god. For what is light in its primordial root but the world-illuminating and life-giving deity? Light is that, which from an abstraction has become a reality. No one has ever seen real or primordial light; what we see is only its broken rays or reflections, which become denser and less luminous as they descend into form and matter. Fire, therefore, is a term which comprehends ALL. Fire is the invisible deity, "the Father", and the manifesting light is God "the Son", and also the Sun. Fire—in the occult sense—is æther, and æther is born of motion, and motion is the eternal dark, invisible Fire. Light sets in motion and controls all in nature, from that highest primordial æther down to the tiniest molecule in Space. MOTION is eternal *per se*, and in the manifested Kosmos it is the Alpha and Omega of that which is called electricity, galvanism, magnetism, sensation —moral and physical—thought, and even life, on this plane. Thus fire, on our plane, is simply the manifestation of motion, or Life.

All cosmic phenomena were referred to by the Rosicrucians as "animated geometry". Every polar function is only a repetition of primeval polarity, said the Fire-Philosophers. For motion begets heat, and æther in motion is heat. When it slackens its motion, then cold is generated, for "cold is æther, in a latent condition". Thus the principal states of nature are three positive and three negative, synthesized by the primeval light. The three negative states are [1] Darkness; [2] Cold; [3] Vacuum or Voidness. The three positive are [1] Light (on our plane) [2] Heat; [3] All nature. Thus Fire may be called the unity of the Universe. Pure cosmic fire (without, so to speak, fuel) is Deity in its universality; for cosmic fire, or heat which it calls forth, is every atom of matter in manifested nature. There is not a thing or a particle in the Universe which does not contain in it latent fire.

Q. Fire, then, may be regarded as the first Element?

A. When we say that fire is the first of the Elements, it is the first only in the visible universe, the fire that we commonly know. Even on the highest plane of our universe, the plane of Globe A or G, fire is in one respect only the fourth. For the Occultist, the Rosecroix of the Middle Ages, and even the mediæval Kabalists, said that to our human perception and even to that of the highest "angels", the universal Deity is darkness, and from this Darkness issues the Logos in the following aspects, [1] Weight [Chaos which becomes æther in its primordial state]; [2] Light; [3] Heat; [4] Fire.

Q. In what relation does the Sun, the highest form of Fire we can recognise, stand to Fire as you have explained it?

A. The Sun, as on our plane, is not even "Solar" fire. The Sun, we see, gives nothing of itself, because it is a reflection; a bundle of electro-magnetic forces, one of the countless milliards of "Knots of Fohat". Fohat is called the "Thread of primeval Light", the "Ball of thread" of Ariadne, indeed, in this labyrinth of chaotic matter. This thread runs through the seven planes tying itself into knots. Every plane being septenary, there are thus forty-nine mystical and physical forces, larger knots forming stars, suns and systems, the smaller planets, and so on.

Q. In what respect is the Sun an illusion?

A. The electro-magnetic knot of our Sun is neither tangible nor dimensional, nor even as molecular as the electricity we know. The Sun absorbs, "psychisizes" and vampirizes its subjects within its system. Further than this it gives out nothing of itself. It is an absurdity, therefore, to say that the solar fires are being consumed and gradually extinguished. The Sun has but one distinct function; it gives the impulse of life to all that breathes and lives under its light. The sun is the throbbing heart of the system; each throb being an impulse. But this heart is invisible: no astronomer will ever see it. That which is concealed in this heart and that which we feel and see, its apparent flame and fires, to use a simile, are the nerves governing the muscles of the solar system, and nerves, moreover, outside of the body. This impulse is not mechanical but a purely spiritual, nervous impulse.

Q. What connection has " weight ", as you use it, with gravity ?

A. By weight, gravity in the occult sense of attraction and repulsion is meant. It is one of the attributes of differentiation, and is a universal property. By attraction and repulsion between matter in various states it is possible, in most cases, to explain (whereas the "law of gravitation" is insufficient to do so) the relation which the tails of the comets assume when nearing the sun; seeing that they manifestly act contrary to this hypothesis.

Q. What is the meaning of water in this connection ?

A. As Water, according to its atomic weight, is composed of one-ninth of Hydrogen (a very inflammable gas, as you know, and without which no organic body is found), and of eight-ninths of Oxygen (which produces combustion when too rapidly combined with any body), what can it be but one of the forms of primordial force or fire, in a cold or latent and fluidic form? Fire bears the same relation to Water as Spirit to Matter.

Sloka (7). BEHOLD, O LANOO, THE RADIANT CHILD OF THE TWO, THE UNPARALLELED REFULGENT GLORY, BRIGHT SPACE, SON OF DARK SPACE, WHO EMERGES FROM THE DEPTHS OF THE GREAT DARK WATERS. IT IS OEAOHOO, THE YOUNGER, THE * * * (*whom thou knowest now as Kwan-Shai-Yin*). HE SHINES FORTH AS THE SUN. HE IS THE BLAZING DIVINE DRAGON OF WISDOM. THE EKA IS CHATUR (*four*), AND CHATUR TAKES TO ITSELF THREE, AND THE UNION PRODUCES THE SAPTA, (*seven*) IN WHOM ARE THE SEVEN WHICH BECOME THE TRIDASA (*the thrice ten*), THE HOSTS AND THE MULTITUDES. BEHOLD HIM LIFTING THE VEIL, AND UNFURLING IT FROM EAST TO WEST. HE SHUTS OUT THE ABOVE AND LEAVES THE BELOW TO BE SEEN AS THE GREAT ILLUSION. HE MARKS THE PLACES FOR THE SHINING ONES (*stars*) AND TURNS THE UPPER SPACE INTO A SHORELESS SEA OF FIRE, AND THE ONE MANIFESTED (*element*) INTO THE GREAT WATERS.

Kwan-Shai-Yin and Kwan-Yin are synonymous with fire and water. The two deities in their primordial manifestation are the dyadic or dual god, bi-sexual nature, Purusha and Prakriti.

Q. What are the terms corresponding to the three Logoi among the words Oeaohoo, the younger, Kwan-Shai-Yin, Kwan-Yin, Father-Mother, Fire and Water, Bright Space and Dark Space ?

A. Everyone must work this out for himself, " Kwan-Shai-Yin marks the places for the shining ones, the stars, and turns the upper space into a shoreless sea of fire, and the one manifested into the great Waters". Think well over this. Fire here stands for the concealed Spirit, Water is its progeny, or moisture, or the creative elements here on earth, the outer crust, and the evolving or creative principles within, or the innermost principles. Illusionists would probably say " above ".

Q. What is the veil which Oeaohoo, the youngest, lifts from East to West ?

A. The veil of reality. It is the curtain which disappears in order to show the spectator the illusions on the stage of Being, the scenery and actors, in short, the universe of MAYA.

Q. What is the " upper space " and " shoreless sea of fire" ?

A. The " upper space " is the space " within ", however paradoxical it may seem, for there is no *above* as no *below* in the infinitude; but the planes follow each other and solidify *from within without*. It is in fact, the universe as it first appears from its *laya* or " zero " state, a shoreless expanse of spirit, or " sea of fire ".

Q. Are the " Great Waters " the same as those on which the Darkness moved "?

A. It is incorrect in this case, to speak of Darkness " moving ". Absolute Darkness, or the Eternal Unknown, cannot be active, and moving *is* action. Even in *Genesis* it is stated that Darkness *was* upon the face of the deep, but that which moved upon the face of the waters, was the " Spirit of God". This means esoterically that in the beginning, when the Infinitude was without form, and Chaos, or the outer Space, was still void, Darkness (*i.e.*, Kalahansa Parabrahm) alone *was*. Then, at the first radiation of Dawn, the " Spirit of God" (after the First and Second Logos were radiated, the Third Logos, or Narayan) began to move on the face of the Great Waters of the " Deep". Therefore the question to be correct, if not clear, should be, " Are the Great Waters the same as the Darkness spoken of ?" The answer would then be in the affirmative. Kalahansa has a dual meaning. Exoterically it is Brahmâ who is the Swan, the " Great Bird", the vehicle in which Darkness manifests itself to human comprehension as light, and this Universe. But esoterically, it is Darkness itself, the unknowable Absolute which is the Source, firstly of the radiation called the First Logos, then of its reflection, the Dawn, or the Second Logos, and finally of Brahmâ, the manifested Light, or the Third Logos. Let us remember, that under this illusion of manifestation, which we see and feel, and which, as we imagine, comes under our sensuous perceptions, is simply and in sober reality, that which we neither hear, see, feel, taste nor touch at all. It is a gross illusion and nothing else.

Q. To return to an early question, in what sense can electricity be called an " entity"?

A. Only when we refer to it as Fohat, its primordial Force. In reality there is only one force, which on the manifested plane appears to us in millions and millions of forms. As said, all proceeds from the one universal primordial fire, and electricity is on our plane one of the most comprehensive aspects of this fire. All contains, and is, electricity, from the nettle which stings to the lightning which kills, from the spark in the pebble to the blood in the body. But the electricity which is seen, for instance, in an electric lamp, is quite another thing from Fohat. Electricity is the cause of the molecular motion in the physical universe, and hence also here, on earth. It is one of the " principles " of matter; for generated as it is in every disturbance of equilibrium, it becomes, so to say, the Kamic element of the object in which this disturbance takes place. Thus Fohat, the primeval cause of this force in its millions of aspects, and as the sum total of universal cosmic electricity, is an " entity".

Q. But what do you mean by this term ? Is not electricity an entity also ?

A. I would not call it so. The word Entity comes from the Latin root *ent*, " being ", of *esse*, " to be "; therefore everything independent of any other thing, is an entity, from a grain of sand up to God. But in our case Fohat is alone an entity, electricity having only a relative significance, if taken in the usual, scientific sense.

Q. Is not cosmic electricity a son of Fohat, and are not his " Seven Sons " Entities?

A. I am afraid not. Speaking of the Sun, we may call it an Entity but we would hardly call a sunbeam that dazzles our eyes, also an Entity. The " Sons of Fohat " are the various Forces having fohatic, or cosmic electric life in their essence or being, and in their various effects. An example: rub amber—a Fohatic Entity—and it will give birth to a " Son " who will attract straws: an apparently inanimate and inorganic object thus manifesting life ! But rub a nettle between your thumb and finger and you will also generate a Son of Fohat, in the shape of a blister. In these cases, the blister is an Entity, but the attraction which draws the straw, is hardly one.

Q. Then Fohat is cosmic electricity and the " Son " is also electricity ?

A. Electricity is the work of Fohat, but as I have just said, Fohat is *not* electricity. From an occult standpoint, electric phenomena are very often produced by the abnormal state of the molecules of an object or of bodies in space: electricity is life and it is death: the first being produced by harmony, the second by disharmony. Vital electricity is under the same laws as Cosmic electricity. The combination of molecules into new forms, and the bringing about of new correlations and disturbance of molecular equilibrium is, in general, the work of, and generates, Fohat. The synthesized principle, or the emanation of the seven cosmic Logoi is beneficent only there where harmony prevails.

Sloka (8). WHERE WAS THE GERM, AND WHERE WAS NOW DARKNESS? WHERE IS THE SPIRIT OF THE FLAME THAT BURNS IN THY LAMP, O LANOO? THE GERM IS THAT, AND THAT IS LIGHT; THE WHITE BRILLIANT SON OF THE DARK HIDDEN FATHER.

Q. Is the spirit of the flame that burns in the lamp of every one of us, our Heavenly Father, or Higher Self?

A. Neither one nor the other; the sentence quoted is merely an analogy and refers to a real lamp which the disciple may be supposed to be using.

Q. Are the elements the bodies of the Dhyan-Chohans, and are Hydrogen, Oxygen, Ozone and Nitrogen, the primordial elements on this plane of matter?

A. The answer to the first part of this question will be found by studying the symbolism of the *Secret Doctrine*.

With regard to the four elements named it is the case; but bear in mind that on a higher plane even volatile ether would appear to be as gross as mud. Every plane has its own denseness of substance or matter its own colours, sounds, dimensions of space, etc., which are quite unknown to us on this plane; and as we have on earth intermediary beings, the ant for instance, a kind of transitional entity between two planes, so on the plane above us there are creatures endowed with senses and faculties unknown to the inhabitants of that plane.

There is a remarkable illustration of Elihu Vedder to the Quatrains of Omar Khayyam, which suggests the idea of the Knots of Fohat. It is the ordinary Japanese representation of clouds, single lines running into knots both in drawings and carvings. It is Fohat the "knot-tier", and from one point of view it is the "world-stuff."

Q. If the Milky Way is a manifestation of this " world-stuff " how is it that it is not seen over the whole sky ?

A. Why should it not be the more contracted, and therefore, its condensed part which alone is seen? This forms into "knots" and passes through the sun-stage, the cometary and planetary stages, until finally it becomes a dead body, or a moon. There are also various kinds of suns. The sun of the solar system is a reflection. At the end of the solar manvantara, it will begin to get less and less radiant, giving less and less heat, owing to a change in the real sun, of which the visible sun is the reflection. After the solar Pralaya, the present sun will, in a future Manvantara, become a cometary body, but certainly not during the life of our little planetary chain. The argument drawn from spectrum star-analysis is not solid, because no account is taken of the passage of light through cosmic dust. This does not mean to say that there is no real difference in the spectra of stars, but that the proclaimed presence of iron or sodium in any particular star may be owing to the modification of the rays of such a star by the cosmic dust with which the earth is surrounded.

Q. Does not the perceptive power of the ant—for instance, the way in which its perceptive faculties differ from our perceptive powers of colour—simply depend upon physiological conditions?

A. The ant can certainly appreciate the sounds that we do, and it can also appreciate sounds that we can never hear, therefore evidently, physiology has nothing whatever to do with the matter. The ant and ourselves possess different degrees of perception. We are on a higher scale of evolution than the ant, but, comparatively speaking, we are the ants to the plane above. . .

Q. When electricity is excited by rubbing amber, is there anything corresponding to an emanation from amber?

A. There is: the electricity which is latent in the amber, exists in everything else, and will be found there if given the appropriate conditions necessary for its liberation. There is one error which is commonly made, than which there can be no greater error in the views of an occultist. A division is made between what you call animate and inanimate objects, as if there could be such a thing as a perfectly inanimate object on earth!

In reality, even that which you call a dead man is more alive than ever. From one point of view, the distinguishing mark between what is called the organic and the inorganic is the function of nutrition, but if there were no nutrition how could those bodies which are called inorganic undergo change? Even crystals undergo a process of accretion, which for them answers the function of nutrition. In reality, as Occult philosophy teaches us, everything which changes is organic; it has the life principle in it, and it has all the potentiality of the higher lives. If, as we say, all in nature is an aspect of the one element, and life is universal, how can there be such a thing as an inorganic atom!

IX.

Meeting held at 17, Lansdowne Road, London, W., on March 7th, 1889; Mr. W. KINGSLAND in the chair.

Sloka (10). FATHER-MOTHER SPIN A WEB WHOSE UPPER END IS FASTENED TO SPIRIT (*Purusha*), THE LIGHT OF THE ONE DARKNESS, AND THE LOWER ONE TO MATTER (*Prakriti*), ITS (*the Spirit's*) SHADOWY END; AND THIS WEB IS THE UNIVERSE SPUN OUT OF THE TWO SUBSTANCES MADE IN ONE, WHICH IS SVABHAVAT.*

Q. Spirit and matter are the opposite ends of the same web; light and darkness, heat and cold, void or space and fulness of all that exists are also opposites. In what sense are these three parts of opposites associated with Spirit and Matter?

A. In the sense in which everything in the universe is associated with either Spirit or Matter, one of these being taken as the permanent element or both. Pure Matter is pure Spirit and cannot be understood even if admitted by our finite intellects. Neither light nor darkness as optical effects, are matter, nor are they spirit, but they are the qualities of the former (matter).

Q. In what relation does Ether stand to Spirit and Matter?

A. Make a difference between Æther and Ether, the former being divine, the latter physical and *infernal*. Ether is the lowest of the septenate division of Akâsa-Pradhâna, primordial Fire-Substance. Æther-Akâsa is the fifth and sixth principles of the body of Kosmos—thus corresponding to Buddhi-Manas, in Man; *Ether* is its Kosmic sediment mingling with the highest layer of the Astral Light. Beginning with the fifth root-race, it will develop fully only at the beginning of the fifth round. Æther is Akâsa in its higher aspect, and *Ether* Akâsa, in its lowest. In one sense it is equivalent to the Father-Creator, Zeus, Pater Æther; on the other to the infernal Serpent-Tempter, the Astral Light of the Kabalists. In the latter case it is fully differentiated matter, in the former only rudimentally differentiated. In other words, Spirit becomes objective matter; and objective matter rebecomes subjective Spirit, when it eludes our metaphysical senses. Æther has the same relation to the Cosmos and our little

Earth, as Manas to the Monad and body. Therefore, Ether has nought to do with Spirit, but a good deal, with subjective matter and our Earth.

Q. "*Brahmâ, as the 'germ of unknown Darkness', is the material from which all evolves and developes.*" *It is one of the axioms of logic that it is impossible for the mind to believe anything of that of which it comprehends nothing. Now if this "material" which is Brahmâ, be formless, then no idea concerning it can enter the mind for the mind can conceive nothing where there is no form. It is the garment or manifestation in the form of "God" which we can perceive, and it is by this and this alone that we can know anything of him. What, therefore, is the first form of this material which human consciousness can recognise?*

A. Your axioms of logic can be applied to the *lower* Manas only and it is from the perceptions of *Kama Manas* alone that you argue. But Occultism teaches only that which it derives from the cognition of the Higher Ego or the *Buddhi Manas*. But, I will try to answer you on your own familiar lines. The first and only form of the *prima materia* our brain-consciousness can cognise, is a circle. Train your thought first of all to a thorough acquaintance with a limited circle, and expand it gradually. You will soon come to a point when without its ceasing to be a circle in thought, it yet becomes infinite and limitless even to the inner perceptions. It is this circle which we call Brahma, the germ, atom or *anu* : a latent atom embracing infinitude and boundless Eternity during Pralaya, an active one during the life-cycles; but one which has neither circumference nor plane, only limitless expansion. Therefore the Circle is the first geometrical figure and symbol in the subjective world, and it becomes a Triangle in the objective. The Triangle is the next figure after the Circle. The first figure, the Circle with the Point, is really no figure ; it is simply a primeval germ, the first thing you can imagine at the beginning of differentiation ; the Triangle must be conceived of once that matter has passed the zero point, or *Layam*. Brahmâ is called an atom, because we have to imagine it as a mathematical point, which, however, can be extended into absoluteness. *Nota Bene*, it is the divine germ and not the atom of the chemists. But beware of the illusion of form. Once you drag down your Deity into human form you limit and condition it, and behold, you have created an anthropomorphic god.

Sloka (11). IT (*the Web*) EXPANDS WHEN THE BREATH OF FIRE (*the Father*) IS UPON IT ; IT CONTRACTS WHEN THE BREATH OF THE MOTHER (*the root of Matter*) TOUCHES IT. THEN THE SONS (*the elements with their respective powers or intelligences*) DISSOCIATE AND SCATTER, TO RETURN INTO THEIR MOTHER'S BOSOM AT THE END OF THE "GREAT DAY" AND REBECOME ONE

WITH HER. WHEN IT (*the Web*) IS COOLING, IT BECOMES RADIANT, ITS SONS EXPAND AND CONTRACT THROUGH THEIR OWN SELVES AND HEARTS; THEY EMBRACE INFINITUDE.*

Q. Is the word "expand" here used in the sense of differentiating or evolving, and "contract" in that of involution, or do these terms refer to Manvantara and Pralaya; or again to a constant vibrating motion of the world-stuff or atoms? Is this expansion and contraction simultaneous or successive?

A. The Web is the ever-existent primordial substance—pure spirit to our conception—the material from which the objective universe or universes are evolved. When the breath of fire or Father, is upon it, it expands; that is to say, as subjective material it is limitless, eternal, indestructible. When the breath of the Mother touches it, that is when the time of manifestation arrives and it has to come into objectivity of form, it contracts, for there is no such thing as an objective material form which is limitless. Though Newton's proposition that every particle of matter has the property of attraction for every other particle, is on the whole correct; and though Leibnitz's proposition that every atom is a universe in itself, and acts through its own inherent force, is also true; yet both are incomplete. For man is also an atom, possessing attraction and repulsion, and is the Microcosm of the Macrocosm. But would it be also true to say that because of the force and intelligence in him he moves independently of every other human unit, or could act and move, unless there were a greater force and intelligence than his own to allow him to live and move in that higher element of Force and Intelligence?

One of the objects of the *Secret Doctrine* is to prove that planetary movements cannot be satisfactorily accounted for by the theory of gravitation alone. Besides the force acting *in* matter there is also a force acting *on* matter.

When we speak of the modified conditions of Spirit-Matter (which is in reality Force), and call them by various names such as heat, cold, light and darkness, attraction and repulsion, electricity and magnetism, &c., &c., to the occultist they are simple names, expressions of difference in manifestations of one and the same Force (always dual in differentiation), but not any specific difference of forces. For all such differences in the objective world result only from the peculiarities of differentiation of matter on which the one free force acts, helped in this by that portion of its essence which we call imprisoned force, or material molecules. The worker within, the inherent force, ever tends to unite with its parent essence without; and

---

* Vol. I., p. 83.

thus, the Mother acting within, causes the Web to contract; and the Father acting without, to expand. Science calls this gravitation; Occultists, the work of the universal Life-Force, which radiates from that Absolute and Unknowable FORCE which is outside of all Space and Time. This is the work of Eternal evolution and involution, or expansion and contraction.

Q. What is the meaning of the phrase "the Web cooling", and when does this take place?

A. Evidently it is itself which is cooling, and not anything outside of itself. When? We are told that it begins when the imprisoned force and intelligence inherent in every atom of differentiated as well as of homogeneous matter arrives at a point when both become the slaves of a higher intelligent Force whose mission it is to guide and shape it. It is the Force which we call the divine Free-Will, represented by the Dhyani-Buddhas. When the centripetal and centrifugal forces of life and being are subjected by the one nameless Force which brings order in disorder, and establishes harmony in Chaos—then it begins cooling. It is impossible to give the exact time in a process the duration of which is unknown.

Q. Is form the result of the interaction of the centrifugal and centripetal forces in matter and nature?

A. Every form, we are told, is built in accordance with the model traced for it in the Eternity and reflected in the DIVINE MIND. There are hierarchies of "Builders of form", and series of forms and degrees, from the highest to the lowest. While the former are shaped under the guidance of the "Builders" the gods "Cosmocratores", the latter are fashioned by the Elementals or Nature Spirits. As an example of this, look at the strange insects and at some reptiles and non-vertebrate creatures, which so closely imitate, not only in their colour but by their outward shape, leaves, flowers, moss-covered branches and other so-called "inanimate" things. Shall we take "natural selection" and the explanations of Darwinists as a solution? I trust not. The theory of natural selection is not only utterly inadequate to explain this mysterious faculty of imitation in the realm of being, but gives also an entirely false conception of the importance of such imitative faculty, as a "potent weapon in the struggle for life". And if this imitative faculty is once proved—as it can easily be—an absolute *misfit* for the Darwinian frame; *i.e.*, if its alleged use, in connection with the so-called "survival of the fittest" is shown to be a speculation which cannot stand close analysis, to what then can the fact of this faculty be attributed? All of you have seen insects which copy with almost a mirror-like fidelity the colour and even outward form of plants, leaves, flowers, pieces of dead twigs, etc. Nor is this a law but rather a frequent exception. What then but an invisible intelligence *outside* the insect can copy with such accuracy from larger originals?

Q. But does not Mr. Wallace show that such imitation has its object in nature? That it is just this which proves the "natural selection" theory, and the innate instinct in the weaker creatures to seek security behind the borrowed garb of certain objects? The insectivora which do not feed upon plants and leaves, will thus leave a leaf-like or moss-like insect safe from attack. This seems very plausible.

A. Very plausible, indeed, if, besides negative facts, there were no very positive evidence to show the unfitness of the natural selection theory to account for the phenomena of imitation. A fact to hold good, must be shown to apply if not universally, then, at any rate, always under the same conditions, *e.g.*, the correspondence and identity of colour between the animals of one and the same locality and the soil of that region would be a general manifestation. But how about the camel of the desert with his coat of the same "protecting" colour as the plains he lives in, and the zebra whose intense, dark stripes *cannot* protect him on the open plains of South Africa, as Mr. Darwin himself admitted. We are assured by Science that this imitation of the colour of the soil is invariably found in the weaker animals, and yet we find the lion—who need fear no stronger enemies than himself in the desert—with a coat that can hardly be distinguished from the rocks and sandy plains he inhabits! We are asked to believe that this "imitation of protecting colours is caused by the use and *benefit* it offers the imitator", as a "potent weapon in the struggle for life"; and yet, daily experience shows to us quite the reverse. Thus, it points to a number of animals in which the most pronounced forms of the imitative faculty are entirely useless, or, worse than that, pernicious and often self-destructive. What good, I ask, is the imitation of human speech to the magpie and parrot—except leading them to be shut up in a cage? Of what use to the monkey its mimicking faculty which brings so many of them to grief and occasionally to great bodily harm and self-destruction; or to a herd of idiotic sheep, in blindly following their leader, even if he happens to tumble down a precipice? This irrepressible desire, also (of *imitating* their leaders) has led more than one unlucky Darwinist, while seeking to prove his favourite hobby, into the most absurdly incongruous statements. Thus, our Hæckelian friend, Mr. Grant Allen, in his work upon the subject under discussion, speaks of a certain Indian lizard blessed with three large parasites of different kinds. Each of these three imitates to perfection the colour of the scales of that part of the body it dwells on: the parasite on the stomach of the creature, is yellow like its stomach; the second parasite having chosen its abode on the back, is as variegated in colour as the dorsal scales; while the third having selected its hermitage on the lizard's brown head, is almost undistinguishable from it in colour. This careful copy of the respective colours, we are told by Mr. G. Allen, is for the purpose of preserving the parasites from the lizard itself. But surely this doughty champion of natural selection does not mean to tell his public that the lizard can see the parasite *on its own head!* Finally, of what use is its brilliant red colour to the fish which lives amidst coral reefs, or to the tiny Birds of Paradise, *colibri*, the rainbow hues of their plumage, imitating all the radiant colours of the tropical fauna and flora—except to make them the more noticeable?

Q. To what causes would Occultism attribute this imitative faculty?

A. To several things. In the case of such rare tropical birds and leaf-like insects to early intermediate links, in the former case between the lizard and the *colibri*, and in the latter between certain vegetations and the insect kind. There was a time, millions of years ago, when such "missing links" were numerous, and on every point of the globe where life was. But now they are becoming with every cycle and generation more rare; they are found at present, only in a limited number of localities, as all such links are relics of the Past.

Q. Will you give us some explanation from the occult standpoint of what is called the "Law of Gravitation"?

A. Science insists that between bodies attraction is directly as the mass and inversely as the square of the distance. Occultists, however, doubt whether this law holds good with regard to the entirety of planetary rotation. Take the first and second laws of Kepler included in the Newtonian law as given by Herschel. "Under the influence of such attractive force mutually urging two spherical gravitating bodies toward one another, they will each, when moving in each other's neighbourhood, be deflected into an orbit concave toward each other, and describe one about the other, regarded as fixed, or both around their common centre of gravity, curves whose forms are limited as those figures known in geometry by the general name of Conic Sections. It will depend upon the particular circumstances or velocity, distance and direction, which of these curves shall be described, whether an ellipse, a circle, a parabola, or an hyperbola, but one or the other it must be . . . . . . &c., &c."

Science says that the phenomena of planetary motion result from the action of two forces, one centripetal, the other centrifugal, and that a body falling to the ground in a line perpendicular to still water does so owing to the law of gravity or of centripetal force. Among others, the following objections brought forward by a learned occultist, may be stated.

[1] That the path of a circle is impossible in planetary motion.

[2] That the argument in the third law of Kepler, namely that "the

squares of the periodic times of any two planets are to each other, in the same proportion as the cubes of their mean distances from the Sun", gives rise to the curious result of a permitted libration in the eccentricities of planets. Now the said forces remaining unchanged in their nature, this can only arise, as he says, " from the interference of an extraneous cause".

[3] That the phenomenon of gravitation or " falling" does not exist, except as the result of a conflict of forces. It can only be considered as an isolated force by way of mental analysis or separation. He asserts, moreover, that the planets, atoms, or particles of matter are not *attracted* towards each other in the direction of right lines connecting their centres, but are forced towards each other in the curves of spirals closing upon the centre of each other. Also that the tidal wave is not the result of attraction. All this, as he shows, results from the conflict of imprisoned and free force; antagonism apparently, but really affinity and harmony.

"Fohat, gathering a few of the clusters of cosmic matter (nebulæ) will, by giving it an impulse, set it in motion anew, develope the required heat, and then leave it to follow its own new growth."*

Q. Is Fohat to be understood as synonymous with force, or that which causes the changing manifestation of matter? If so, how can Fohat be said to " leave it to follow its own new growth", when all growth depends upon the indwelling force?

A. All growth depends upon the indwelling force, because on this plane of ours it is this force alone which acts consciously. The universal force cannot be regarded as a conscious force as we understand the word consciousness, because it would immediately become a personal god. It is only that which is enclosed in form, a limitation of matter, which is conscious of itself on this plane. This Free Force or Will, which is limitless and absolute, cannot be said to act understandingly, but it is the one and sole immutable Law of Life and Being.

Fohat, therefore, is spoken of as the synthetic motor power of all the imprisoned life-forces and the medium between the absolute and conditioned Force. It is a link, just as Manas is the connecting link between the gross matter of the physical body and the divine Monad which animates it, but is powerless to act upon the former directly.

Q. If Force is a unity or One, manifesting in an unlimited variety of ways, it is difficult to understand the statement in the Commentary that: " There is heat internal and external in every atom" ; i.e., latent and active heat or dynamic and kinetic heat. Heat is the phenomenon of a perception of matter actuated by force in a peculiar manner. Heat, therefore, on the physical plane is simply matter in motion. If there is heat in a more interior and occult sense than physical heat, it must be perceived by some higher and more interior senses by virtue of its activities on whatever plane it

---

* Vol. I., p. 84.

manifests. For this perception three conditions are necessary, an actuating force, a form which is actuated and that which perceives the form in motion. The terms "latent", "potential" or "dynamic" heat are misnomers, because heat, whether on the first or the seventh plane of consciousness, is the perception of matter or substance in motion.

Is the discrepancy between the above statement and the teaching of the "Secret Doctrine" apparent or real?

A. Why should heat on any other plane than ours be the perception of matter or substance in motion? Why should an occultist accept the condition of [1] the actuating force; [2] the form which is actuated; [3] that which perceives the form in motion, as those of heat?

As with every ascending plane heterogeneity tends more and more to homogeneity, so on the seventh plane the form will disappear, there being nothing to be actuated, the acting Force will remain in solitary grandeur, to perceive but itself; or in Spencer's phraseology, it will have become both "subject and object, the perceiver and the perceived". The terms used are not contradictory, but symbols borrowed from physical science in order to render occult action and processes more clear to the minds of those who are trained in that science. In fact, each of these specifications of heat and force, corresponds to one of the principles in man.

The "heat centres", from the physical standpoint, would be the zero-point, because they are spiritual.

The word "perceived" is somewhat erroneous, it should rather be "sensed". Fohat is the agent of the law, its representative, the representative of the Manasa-putras, whose collectivity is—the eternal mind.

Q. In the passage of a globe into Pralaya does it remain in situ, i.e., still forming part of a planetary chain and maintaining its proper position in relation to the other globes? Does the dissociation by means of heat play any part in the passage of a globe into Pralaya?

A. This is explained in "Esoteric Buddhism". When a globe of a planetary chain goes into "obscuration" every quality, including heat, retires from it and it remains *in statu quo*, like the "sleeping Beauty", until Fohat, the "Prince Charmant", awakens it with a kiss.

Q. The sons are spoken of as dissociating and scattering. This appears to be opposed to the action of returning to their "mother's bosom" at the end of the "Great Day". Does the dissociating and scattering refer to the formation of the globe from the universally diffused world-stuff, in other words emerging from Pralaya?

A. The dissociating and scattering refers to Nitya Pralaya. This is an eternal and perpetual Pralaya which is taking place ever since there were globes and differentiated matter. It is simply atomic change.

Q. What is meant by the expression expanding and contracting through their own " selves and hearts " and how is this connected with the last line of the sloka, " They embrace Infinitude ".

A. This has already been explained. Through their own inherent and imprisoned force they strive collectively to join the one universal or free force, that is to say, embrace infinitude, this free force being infinite.

Q. What is the relation between electricity and physical or animal magnetism and hypnotism ?

A. If by electricity, you mean the science which unfolds on this plane, and under a dozen various qualifications the phenomena and laws of the electric fluid—then I answer, none at all. But if you refer to the electricity we call *Fohatic*, or *intra*-cosmic, then I will say that all these forms of phenomena are based on it.

X.

Meeting held at 17, Lansdowne Road, London, W., on March 14th, 1889;

MR. W. KINGSLAND *in the chair.*

STANZA IV.

Sloka (1.) LISTEN, YE SONS OF THE EARTH, TO YOUR INSTRUCTORS—THE SONS OF THE FIRE. LEARN THERE IS NEITHER FIRST NOR LAST; FOR ALL IS ONE NUMBER, ISSUED FROM NO NUMBER.

Q. Are the sons of the Fire, the Rays of the Third Logos ?

A. The "Rays" are the "Sons of the Fire mist", produced by the *Third Creation*, or Logos. The actual "Sons of the Fire" of the Fifth Race and Sub-races are so called simply because they by their wisdom belong, or are nearer to, the hierarchy of the divine "Sons of the Fire-Mist", the highest of the planetary Chohans or Angels. But the Sons of the Fire here spoken of as addressing the Sons of the Earth are, in this case, the King-Instructors who incarnated on this earth to teach nascent Humanity. As "Kings" they belong to the divine dynasties of which every nation, India, Chaldea, Egypt, Homeric Greece, &c., has preserved a tradition or record in some form or other. The name "Sons of the Fire-Mist" was also given to the Hierophants of old. They are certainly sub-divisions of the Third Logos. They are the Fire-Chohans or Angels, the Ether Angels, the Air and Water Angels, and the Angels of the Earth. The seven lower Sephiroth are the earthly angels and correspond to the seven hierarchies of the seven elements, five of which are known, and two unknown.

Q. Do they, then, correspond to the Races ?

A. They do. Otherwise where would be the intellectual Races with brains and thought, if it was not for these hierarchies that incarnated in them ?

Q. What is the distinction between these various Hierarchies ?

A. In reality these fires are not separate, any more than are the souls or monads to him who sees beyond the veil of matter or illusion.

He who would be an occultist must not separate either himself or anything else from the rest of creation or *non-creation*. For, the moment he distinguishes himself from even a vessel of dishonour, he will not be able to join himself to any vessel of honour. He must think of himself as an infinitesimal something, not even as an individual atom, but as a part of the world-atoms as a whole, or become an illusion, a nobody, and vanish like a breath leaving no trace behind. As illusions, we are separate distinct bodies, living in masks furnished by Maya. Can we claim one single atom in our body as distinctly our own? Everything, from spirit to the tiniest particle, is part of the whole, at best a link. Break a single link and all passes into annihilation; but this is impossible. There is a series of vehicles becoming more and more gross, from spirit to the densest matter, so that with each step downward and outward we get more and more the sense of separateness developed in us. Yet this is illusory, for if there were a real and complete separation between any two human beings, they could not communicate with, or understand each other in any way.

Thus with these hierarchies. Why should we separate their classes in our mind, except for purposes of distinction in *practical* Occultism, which is but the lowest form of applied Metaphysics. But if you seek to separate them on this plane of illusion, then all I can say is, that there exists between these Hierarchies the same abysses of distinction as between the " principles " of the Universe or those of man, if you like, and the same " principles " in a bacillus.

" There is a passage in the Bhagavad-Gita (ch. viii.) wherein Krishna, speaking symbolically and esoterically, says: ' I will state the times (conditions) . . . . at which devotees departing (from this life) do so never to return (be reborn). The Fire, the Flame, the day, the bright (lucky fortnight), the six months of the Northern solstice (dying) in these those who know the Brahman (Yogis) go to the Brahman. Smoke, Night, the dark (unlucky) fortnight, the six months of the southern solstice, (dying) in these, the devotee goes to the lunar light (or mansion, the astral light also) and returns (is reborn)."*

Q. What is the explanation of this passage?

A. It means that the devotees are divided into two classes, those who reach Nirvana on Earth, and either accept or refuse it (though never to be born again, in this *Mahakalpa*, or age of Brahmâ); and those who do not reach this state of bliss as Buddha and others did.

" The Fire, the Flame, the day, the bright fortnight of the moon ", are all symbols of the highest absolute deity. Those who die in such a state of absolute purity, go to Brahman, *i.e.*, have a right to Moksha or Nirvana. On the other hand " Smoke, night, the dark fortnight, &c.", are all symbolical of matter, the darkness of ignorance. Those who die in such a state of incomplete purification, must of course be reborn. Only the homogeneous, the absolutely purified unalloyed spirit, can be re-united to the Deity or go to Brahma.

Sloka (2). LEARN WHAT WE, WHO DESCEND FROM THE PRIMORDIAL SEVEN, WE WHO ARE BORN FROM THE PRIMORDIAL FLAME, HAVE LEARNED FROM OUR FATHERS.

"The first 'Primordial' are the highest beings on the scale of existence. The 'Primordial' proceed from 'Father-Mother'"*

Q. Is Father-Mother here synonymous with the Third Logos?

A. The first primordial seven are born from the Third Logos. This is before it is differentiated into the Mother, when it becomes pure primordial matter in its first primitive essence, Father-Mother potentially. Mother becomes the immaculate mother only when the differentiation of spirit and matter is complete. Otherwise there would exist no such qualification. No one would speak of pure spirit as immaculate, for it cannot be otherwise. The mother is, therefore, the immaculate matter before it is differentiated under the breath of the pre-cosmic Fohat, when it becomes the "immaculate mother" of the "Son" or the manifested Universe, in form. It is the latter which begins the hierarchy that will end with Humanity or man.

Sloka (3). FROM THE EFFULGENCY OF LIGHT—THE RAY OF THE EVER-DARKNESS—SPRING IN SPACE THE RE-AWAKENED ENERGIES (*Dhyan-Chohans*): THE ONE FROM THE EGG, THE SIX AND THE FIVE; THEN THE THREE, THE ONE, THE FOUR, THE ONE, THE FIVE, THE TWICE SEVEN, THE SUM TOTAL. AND THESE ARE: THE ESSENCES, THE FLAMES, THE ELEMENTS, THE BUILDERS, THE NUMBERS, THE ARUPA, (*formless*), THE RUPA (*with bodies*), AND THE FORCE OR DIVINE MAN—THE SUM TOTAL. AND FROM THE DIVINE MAN EMANATED THE FORMS, THE SPARKS, THE SACRED ANIMALS, AND THE MESSENGERS OF THE SACRED FATHERS (*the Pitris*) WITHIN THE HOLY FOUR.

Q. Can you explain these numbers and give their meaning?

A. As said in the Commentary, we are not at present concerned in the process, that is to say, it cannot at present be made public. Some few

---

* Vol i., p. 88.

hints, however, may be given. The Rabbins call the Circle (or as some say, the first Point in it) Echod, the ONE, or Ain-Soph. On a lower plane, the fourth, it becomes Adam Kadmon, the manifested seven and the unmanifested ten, or the complete Sephirothal Tree. The Sephiroth, therefore, are the same as the Elohim. Now the name of the latter written in Hebrew, Alhim, is composed of five letters; and these letters in their values in numerals, being placed round a circle can be transmuted at will, as they could not be were they applied to any other geometrical figure. The circle is endless, that is to say, has neither beginning nor end. Now the literal Kabala is divided into three parts or methods, the third of which is called Temura or permutation. According to certain rules one letter or numeral is substituted for another. The Kabalistic alphabet is divided into two equal parts, each letter or numeral of one part corresponding to a like number or letter in the other part. By changing the letters alternately, twenty-two permutations or combinations are produced, which process is called Tziruph.

The footnote on pages 90 and 91 (Vol. 1, *Secret Doctrine*), makes my meaning quite clear.

Sloka (4.) THIS WAS THE ARMY OF THE VOICE—THE DIVINE SEPTENARY. THE SPARKS OF THE SEVEN ARE SUBJECT TO, AND THE SERVANTS OF, THE FIRST, THE SECOND, THIRD, FOURTH, FIFTH, SIXTH AND THE SEVENTH OF THE SEVEN. THESE ("*Sparks*") ARE CALLED SPHERES, TRIANGLES, CUBES, LINES; AND MODELLERS: FOR THUS STANDS THE ETERNAL NIDANA—THE OI-HA-HOU (*the permutation of Oeaohoo*).

Q. What are the "Life-Winds" in the commentary [page 96]?

A. The Life-winds are the various modes of out-breathing and in-breathing, changing thereby the polarity of the body and states of consciousness. It is Yoga practice, but beware of taking the exoteric works on Yoga literally. They all require a key.

Q. What is the meaning of the sentence beginning "The Sparks, etc." (vide supra)?

A. The sparks mean the Rays as well to the lower intelligence as to the human sparks or Monads. It relates to the circle and the digits, and is equivalent to saying that the figures 31415 as given on page 90 and 91, are all subject to the circumference and diameter of the circle.

Q. Why is Sarasvati (the goddess of speech) also called the goddess af esoteric wisdom? If the explanation lies in the meaning of the word Logos, why is there a distinction between the immovable mind and movable speech? Is mind equivalent to Mahat, or to the Higher and Lower Manas?

A. The question is rather a complicated one. Saraswati, the Hindu goddess, is the same as Vâch, whose name means Speech and who is the female Logos, esoterically. The second question seems rather involved. I believe it is because the Logos or Word is called the incarnate wisdom, "Light shining in darkness". The distinction lies between the immovable or eternal immutable ALL, and the movable Speech or Logos, *i.e.*, the periodical and the manifested. It can relate to the Universal, and to the individual mind, to Mahat, or to the Higher Manas, or even to the lower, the Kama Manas or Brain-Mind. Because that which is desire, instinctive impulse in the lower, becomes thought in the Higher. The former finds expression in acts, the latter in words. Esoterically, thought is more responsible and punishable than act. But exoterically it is the reverse. Therefore, in ordinary human law, an assault is more severely punished than the thought or intention, *i.e.*, the threat, whereas *Karmically* it is the contrary.

Q. "God geometrizes", says Plato, but seeing that there is no personal God, how is it that the process of formation is by Dots, Lines, Triangles, Cubes, Circles, and finally Spheres ? And how when the sphere leaves the static state, does the inherent force of Breath set it whirling ?

A. The term "God"—unless referring to the Unknown Deity or *Absoluteness*, which can hardly be supposed *acting* in any way—has always meant in ancient philosophies the collectivity of the working and intelligent Forces in nature. The word "Forest" is singular, yet it is the term to express the idea of thousands or even millions of trees of different kinds. Materialists have the option of saying " Nature ", or still better— "Law geometrizes" if they so prefer. But in the days of Plato, the average reader would hardly have understood the metaphysical distinction and real meaning. The truth, however, of Nature ever " geometrizing " is easily ascertained. Here is an instance : Heat is the modification of the motions or particles of matter. Now, it is a physical and mechanical law that particles or bodies in motion on themselves, assume a spheroidal form —this, from a globular planet down to a drop of rain. Observe the snow-flakes, which along with crystals exhibit to you all the geometrical forms existing in nature. As soon as motion ceases, the spheroidal shape alters; or, as Tyndall tells us, it becomes a flat drop, then the drop forms an equilateral triangle, a hexagon and so on. In observing the breaking up of ice-particles in a large mass, through which he passed heat rays, he observed that the first shape the particles assumed, was triangular or pyramidal, then cubical and finally hexagonal, &c. Thus, even modern physical science, corroborates Plato and justifies his proposition.

Q. When Tyndall took a large block of ice and threw a powerful ray upon it and thence on to a screen, there were to be seen the forms of ferns and plants in it. What is the reason of this?

A. This question ought really to be addressed first to Professor Tyndall, who would give a scientific explanation of it—and perhaps he has already done so. But Occultism would explain it by saying either that the ray helped to show the astral shapes which were preparing to form future ferns and plants, or that the ice had preserved the reflection of actual ferns and plants that had been reflected in it. Ice is a great magician, whose occult properties are as little know as those of Ether. It is occultly connected with the astral light, and may under certain conditions, reflect certain images from the invisible astral region, just as light and a sensitised plate may be made to reflect stars that cannot be perceived even by the telescope. This is well known to learned Yogis who dwell on the eternal ice of Bodrinath and the Himalayas. At any rate, ice has certainly the property of retaining images of things impressed on its surface under certain conditions of light, images which it preserves invisibly until it is melted. Fine steel has the same property, though it is of a less occult nature. Were you to observe the ice from the surface, these forms would not be seen. But once that in decomposing the ice with heat you deal with the forces and the things that were impressed on it, then you find that it throws off these images and the forms appear. It is but one link leading to another link. All this is not modern science of course, yet it is fact and truth.

Q. Do numbers and geometrical figures represent to human consciousness the laws of action in the Divine Mind?

A. They do, most assuredly. There is no chance evolution or formation, nor is any so-called abnormal appearance or cosmic phenomenon due to haphazard circumstances.

(*Sloka 5.*) "DARKNESS," THE BOUNDLESS OR THE NO-NUMBER, ADI-NIDANA SVABHAVAT: THE O (*for x, unknown quantity*).

I. THE ADI-SANAT, THE NUMBER, FOR HE IS ONE.
II. THE VOICE OF THE WORD, SVABHAVAT, THE NUMBERS, FOR HE IS ONE AND NINE.
III. THE "FORMLESS SQUARE" (*Arupa*).

AND THESE ENCLOSED WITHIN THE O (*Boundless Circle*), ARE THE SACRED FOUR, AND THE TEN ARE THE ARUPA (*subjective, formless*) UNIVERSE; THEN COME THE "SONS", THE SEVEN FIGHTERS, THE ONE, THE EIGHTH LEFT OUT, AND HIS BREATH WHICH IS THE LIGHT-MAKER (*Bhâskara*).

Q. The "One Rejected" is the sun of our system. Astronomically is there any explanation of Mârttanda's rejection?

A. The sun is older than any of its planets—though younger than the moon. Its "rejection" means that when bodies or planets began to form, helped by its rays, magnetic radiance or heat, and especially by its magnetic attraction, it had to be stopped, otherwise it would have swallowed all the younger bodies like as Saturn is fabled to have treated his progeny. This does not mean that all the planets are thrown out from the sun, as modern Science teaches, but simply that under the Rays of the sun they acquire their growth. Aditi is the ever-equilibrizing mother-nature on the purely spiritual and subjective plane. She is the Sakti, the female power or potency of the fecundating spirit; and it is for her to regulate the behaviour of the sons born in her bosom. The Vedic allegory is very suggestive.

Q. Were all the planets in our solar system first comets and then suns?

A. They were not suns in our, or their present solar systems, but comets in space. All began life as wanderers over the face of the infinite Kosmos. They detached themselves from the common storehouse of already prepared material, the Milky Way (which is nothing more or less than the quite developed world-stuff, all the rest in space being the crude material, as yet invisible to us); then, starting on their long journey they first settled in life where conditions were prepared for them by Fohat, and gradually became suns. Then each sun, when its Pralaya arrived, was resolved into millions and millions of fragments. Each of these fragments moved to and fro in space collecting fresh materials, as it rolled on, like an avalanche, until it came to a stop through the laws of attraction and repulsion, and became a planet in our own, as in other systems, beyond our telescopes. The sun's fragments will become just such planets after the Solar pralaya. It was a comet once upon a time, in the beginning of Brahmâ's Age. Then it came to its present position, whence it will burst asunder, and its atoms will be whirled into space for æons, and æons like all other comets and meteors, until each, guided by Karma, is caught in the vortex of the two forces, and fixed in some higher and better system.

Thus the Sun will live in his children as a portion of the parents lives in their offspring. When that day comes, the semblance or reflection of the Sun which we see, will first fall off like a veil from the face of the true Sun. No mortal will see it, for no mortal eye could bear its radiance Were this veil once removed for even a second, all the planets of its system would be instantaneously reduced to ashes, as the sixty thousand of King Sagara's Sons *were destroyed by a* glance of Kapila's eye.

Sloka (6.) THEN THE SECOND SEVEN, WHO ARE THE LIPIKA, PRODUCED BY THE THREE (*Word, Voice and Spirit*). THE REJECTED SUN IS ONE, THE "SONS-SUNS" ARE COUNTLESS.

Q. *What is the relation of the Lipika, the " Second Seven" to the " Primordial Seven" and to the first " Sacred Four" ?*

A. If you believe that any, save the highest Initiates, can explain this to your satisfaction, then you are greatly mistaken. The relation can be better understood, or rather, shown to be above all understanding, by first studying the Gnostic systems of the early centuries of Christianity, from that of Simon Magus down to the highest and noblest of them, the so-called PISTIS-SOPHIA. All these systems are derived from the East. That which we call the " Primordial Seven" and the " Second Seven" are called by Simon Magus the Æons, the primeval, the second and the third series of Syzygies. They are the graduated emanations, ever descending lower and lower into matter, from that primordial principle which he calls Fire, and we, Svâbhâvat. Behind that Fire, the manifested but silent Deity, stands with him as it does with us, that " which is, was, and ever will be". Let us compare his system with ours.

In a passage quoted from his works by the author of *Philosophumena*, we read :—" From this permanent Stability and Immortality of this first manifested principle ' Fire' (the third Logos) which immutability does not preclude activity, as the second from it is endowed with intelligence and reason (Mahat), it (the Fire) passed from the potentiality of action to action itself. From this series of evolutions were formed six beings, or the emanation from the infinite potency; they were formed in Syzygies, *i.e.*, they radiated out of the flame two by two, one being active, the other the passive principle ". These Simon named Nous and Epinoia, or Spirit and Thought Phône and Onoma, Voice and Name, and Logismos and Euthumêsis, Reasoning and Reflection. And again :—" In each of these six primitive Beings the Infinite Potency was in its totality; but it was there in potentiality and not in act. It had to be established therein through an image (that of the paradigm), in order that it should appear in all its essence, virtue, grandeur and effects; for only then could it become like unto the Parent Potency nfinite and eternal. If, on the contrary, it was not conformed by or through the Image, that Potentiality could never become Potency or pass into action, but was lost for lack of use, as it happens to a man who having an aptitude for grammar or geometry does not exercise it ; it gets lost for him just as if he never had it " (*Philosophumena*, p. 250).

He shows that whether these Æons belong to the superior, middle or lower world, they are all one, except in material density, which determines their outward manifestations and the result produced, not their real essence which is one, or their mutual relations which, as he says, are established from eternity by immutable laws.

Now the first, the second, third or primordial seven or Lipika, are all one. When they emanate from one plane to another, it is a repetition of—"as above, so below". They are all differentiated in matter or density, not in qualities; the same qualities descend on to the last plane, our own, where man is endowed with the same potentiality, if he but knew how to develop it, as the highest Dhyan-Chohans.

In the hierarchies of Æons, Simon gives three pairs of two each, the seventh being the fourth which descends from one plane to another.

The Lipika proceed from Mahat and are called in the Kabala the four Recording Angels; in India, the four Maharajahs, those who record every thought and deed of man; they are called by St. John in the Revelation, the Book of Life. They are directly connected with Karma and what the Christians call the Day of Judgment, in the East it was called the Day after Mahamanvantara, or the "Day-Be-With-Us". Then everything becomes one, all individualities are merged into one, yet each knowing itself, a mysterious teaching indeed. But then, that which to us now is non-consciousness or the unconscious, will then be absolute consciousness.

Q, *What relation have the Lipika to Mahat ?*

A. They are a division, four taken from one of the Septenates that emanates from Mahat. Mahat corresponds with the Fire of Simon Magus, the secret and the manifested Divine Ideation, made to witness to itself in this objective Universe through the intelligent forms we see around us, in what is called creation. Like all other emanations, they are "Wheels within Wheels". The Lipika are on the plane corresponding to the highest plane of our chain of globes.

Q. *What is the difference between Spirit, Voice and Word ?*

A. The same as between Atma, Buddhi and Manas, in one sense. Spirit emanates from the unknown Darkness, the mystery into which none of us can penetrate. That Spirit—call it the "Spirit of God" or Primordial Substance—mirrors itself in the Waters of Space—or the still undifferentiated matter of the future Universe—and produces thereby the first flutter of differentiation in the homogeneity of primordial matter. This is the Voice, pioneer of the "Word" or the first manifestation; and from that Voice emanates the Word or Logos, that is to say, the definite and objective expression of that which has hitherto remained in the depths of the Concealed Thought. That which mirrors itself in Space is the Third Logos. We may express this Trinity also by the terms Colour, Sound, and Numbers,

LONDON:
WOMEN'S PRINTING SOCIETY, LIMITED,
GREAT COLLEGE STREET, WESTMINSTER, S.W.

[The following is reproduced from *Lucifer*, Nov. 15, 1889 (5:27), p. 178. — TUP]

NOTICE TO THOSE INTERESTED IN THE "TRANSACTIONS OF THE BLAVATSKY LODGE."

THE discussions on the first volume of the *Secret Doctrine* which have been reported by a stenographer were of so difficult a nature that much of the substance, as it stands, is entirely useless. The revision and rewording of these reports, which had to be undertaken by one of the busiest of the 17 Lansdowne Road household, is progressing; but it has to be again revised and prepared for press, and this no one can do but H. P. B.; owing, however, to her multifarious duties the work can progress but slowly. It is to be hoped that the anxiety of our friends will be relieved by the above explanation.

G. R. S. MEAD,
Sec., "Blavatsky Lodge."

INDEX

Abel
  symbolizes separation of the sexes II 8
Absolute, The, ch 1-3 passim
  is dormant, latent mind I 18
  we can never approach I 19
  is never differentiated I 26
  radiation from II 10
Adam Kadmon I 43-4; II 7-8, 42
Adepts I 57, 60, 64
  classification of I 55
Æon(s) I 9-10; II 46-7
Ah-hi I 17-24, 45
  are the highest dhyānis I 18
  belong to the three planes I 20-1
  have been men I 21-3
Ahura-Mazda I 15
Ain-Soph I 9, 60; II 42
  IT is, in Kabbala I 4
  Sephīrāh emanates from I 4-5
Ākāśa I 14, 24; II 19, 30
  and astral light I 53; II 10-12
  universal element II 15
Alaya I 24; II 5
  means "Soul of the World," *Anima Mundi* I 44-5
Anima Mundi I 6, 44-5; II 5
  Architect of the Universe I 41
Animal Life
  imitative colors in, explained II 34-5
Ant I 12-13; II 29
Astral Light, Plane I 23, 42; II 19, 30, 40, 44
  relation of, to memory I 53
  and ākāśa I 53; II 10-12
  action of, on man I 53-4
  and dreams I 58
  māyā II 7-8
Ātma I 20, 24, 51; II 47
  in human principles corresponds to Parabrahm I 5
Atom(s) I 8, 22; II 17, 24, 29, 31-3, 36, 40, 45
  indestructible II 5
  the real, does not exist on material plane II 19-20
Atonement, basis of doctrine of I 55-6

Brahman, Brahmā I 3-5, 14, 42; II 13, 18, 20, 31, 40-1
  in *Vishnu Purāna* I 31
  different aspects of I 44
  an aspect of the divine mind II 5-6
  human conception of II 26-7

Buddhi I 5, 14, 20, 51-2; II 30-1, 47
  different uses of term I 7, 24
Builders I 33; II 6, 11, 33, 41
  grades of I 39-41
  Sons of Manvantaric Dawn I 45-6

Cerebellum I 59
  instinctual mind and I 23, 27
  functions in sleep I 28-9
Chaos I 14, 36; II 9-10, 15, 24, 26, 33
  Gaea springs from, preceding Eros I 4
Christ, Christian(ity) I 3, 32, 56, 60; II 6, 46
Circle I 5, 14; II 3-5, 35, 42-4
  symbology of, and triangle II 31
Clairvoyant I 29, 56-8, 63; II 11
  sight of I 37-8
Consciousness I 5-6, 9, 12, 14-16, 18-25, 28-9, 34, 36, 44, 52-64; II 11-14, 36
  what is I 24-5
Cosmocratores I 40-1; II 6, 33
Crookes, Prof. [William] I 6-8

Daivīprakriti I 33
Darkness I 20, 45; II 3-4, 8, 11, 15, 17, 23-4, 28, 30-1, 41, 43-4, 47
  meaning of, in Stanza I, I 30-1
  and Light are metaphorical I 36
  Great Waters same as II 26
Death I 25, 31, 42, 55, 61-3; II 28
Devachan I 59, 61, 63
  no conception of time in I 15-16
Dhyān-Chohan I 33, 45, 54; II 11, 18, 39, 41, 47
  defined I 39-40; II 12-13, 28
Dhyāni-Buddhas
  defined I 40-4; II 12-14
Dreams I 23, 27-8, 49-64
  nature of I 16
  principles active in I 49-52
  real I 50-1
  action of karma in I 55
  prophetic I 56-7, 59
  do Adepts dream? I 57
  of animals I 57
  explained I 58-9
  linga śarīra during I 62
  reaching devachanee in I 63
  seven classes of I 64
Duration I 9-12, 14-15; II 9

Egg I 13; II 18-19, 41
  Mundane, Virgin, & eternal II 3-5, 15-16

Electricity II 23-4, 32
  root of, is the One Life II 5-6
  and Fohat II 27-8
  exists in everything II 29
  relation to magnetism & hypnotism II 38
Element(s) I 8; II 12, 20, 22-6, 31, 39, 41
  all substances from root I 47
  water the first cosmic II 15
  on different planes II 28-9
Elementals II 33
  relation of elements to II 12, 15
Elohīm II 42
  of Jews, are the Seven Logoi emanated by the *Son* I 5
Emanation I 4, 18, 20, 54; II 28, 46-7
  versus radiation II 10
Ether
  contains elements II 15
  is, molecular? II 19
  defined II 30

Father-Mother I 32-3; II 9, 26, 30, 41
Father, Mother, Son (see Logos, Logoi)
  meanings of I 30-3; II 9
Fire I 34, 47; II 15, 30-2, 39-41, 46-7
  various meanings of II 23-7
Fohat II 11, 24
  many senses of I 33
  is the force of the divine mind II 5
  meaning of word II 6
  primordial force of electricity II 27-8
  is, synonymous with force? II 36-8

Germ II 17, 19, 28, 31
  a figurative expression II 3-5
Globe(s) I 39, 42-4, 46; II 19, 24, 47
  obscuration of II 37
Gnostic(ism) I 32; II 11, 46
God(s) I 3-4, 15, 27, 40, 56, 60; II 5, 13, 20-1, 26, 43, 47
  why occultists do not worship I 43-4
Gravity
  connection of "weight" with II 25
  does not fully explain movement of planets II 32-3
  explanation of law of II 35-6
Great Breath I 9-10; II 6

Heat II 23-4, 29, 32, 43, 45
  there is internal and external, in every atom II 36-7
Hermes Trismegistus I 5

Immaculate Conception, Mother
  meaning of II 6, 7, 41
Insects I 12-13, 57
  which imitate leaves, etc. II 33-5

Īśvara I 13
It
  nothing can proceed from I 4

Jīvanmukta, powers of a I 55
Jupiter, superior to Earth I 41

Kalahansa, dual meaning of II 26
Karma I 55; II 13, 45, 47
Kriyā-śakti, power of I 51
Kwan-Shai-Yin, Kwan-Yin II 25-6

Laya I 10, 32-3, 36, 45; II 26, 31
  denotes a state or condition I 6-8; II 16
Light (see Astral Light) I 4, 33, 36; II 7, 13, 17-18, 22-3, 30, 41, 44
  used in dual sense I 30-1
Lipika
  relation of, to Primordial Seven and Mahat II 46-7
Logos, Logoi I 17-18, 35, 44; II 8, 13, 17, 24, 28, 42-3, 47
  1st manifested, proceeds from unmanifested I 3-6
  1st, 2nd, and 3rd I 13-14
  the three, correspond to ātma, buddhi, and manas I 20
  or Father, Mother, and Son I 30-3
  symbols for the three II 3-5
  1st, after 7th eternity II 9-11
  correlations of the three II 26-7
  is Father-Mother the 3rd? II 39, 41

Mahat I 5-7, 54; II 6-7, 9, 11, 13, 42-3, 46-7
  explained I 14, 19, 24, 41-2
Man I 20; II 6, 41
  thinking, lives on seven planes I 59-60
Manas I 5, 14, 40; II 13, 30-1, 36, 42-3, 47
  higher, and lower, compared I 23-4, 49-52, 55-6
Mānasaputras I 21-2, 24; II 11, 37
  inspire lower manas I 54-6
Manu I 44; II 13-15, 20
Manvantara I 9-10, 18, 20-1, 26, 33-5, 45; II 11, 20, 29, 32, 47
  defined II 13-15
Mātri-Padma, the eternal Egg II 3, 5
Matter I 5-8, 10, 12, 24, 27, 32, 40, 50; II 3-5, 9, 17, 19, 22, 36, 41, 47
  two kinds of II 6
  relation between spirit, and ether II 30-3
Māyā I 12, 15, 30; II 5, 7-8, 40
  awakens Nidānas I 25-6
  different conceptions of I 26-7
Mediumship, some dangers of I 62-3
Milky Way
  is, atomic? II 18-19

Milky Way (cont.)
   matter of the II 22-3, 45
   why, not over whole sky II 28-9
Mind I 6, 41, 49, 54, 60-1; II 21, 37, 43
   Cosmic, Divine, and Universal I 17-20, 24-5; II 5-6, 10-11, 14, 44
   waking, sleeping, & instinctual I 23, 27
"Missing Links," were once numerous II 35
Mother-Father I 4-5, 13-14, 21
   matter is root of "mother" II 6
Mūlaprakriti
   conceals Parabrahm I 4, 35; II 3
   means root of nature or matter I 5, 7
   is Aditi of the Vedas I 6
Mundane Egg
   expression of Abstract Form II 3-5

Nārāyana I 13; II 26
Naros I 9
Natural Selection Theory
   defects of II 33-5
Nature I 17, 26, 35, 41, 45; II 24, 43, 45
   no inanimate II 29
Neith (Egy), and first emanation I 4
Nidāna(s) I 34; II 42, 44
   defined I 25-6
Nirvāna I 12, 25-6, 34, 42, 55, 60; II 40
Number(s), why used in Stanzas II 21

Parabrahm I 9, 42
   the *Rootless Root* of all I 4-5
   is not a cause I 35
   the Ever-Darkness II 3, 17, 26
Pistis Sophia II 46
Planetary Spirit(s) I 21; II 39
   explained I 39-44
Planet(s), Planetary I 32, 39-42, 46; II 8, 11, 14, 19, 22, 24, 29, 36-7, 45
Plato, Platonic I 5; II 21, 43
   method in education I 48
Point II 19, 42
   in circle and Mundane Egg I 14; II 3-4, 7
Pradhāna I 14; II 30
Pralaya I 8-10, 17-18, 26, 31-2, 34, 42-3, 45; II 6, 20, 29, 31-2, 37, 45
Privation (Aristotle) I 5; II 12
Protyle (Crookes) I 6-8; II 7
Pythagoras, Pythagorean I 20; II 3, 21
   triangle and square II 7-8, 18

Sarasvatī
   goddess of esoteric wisdom? II 42-3
Sat I 17, 20; II 6
   is not existence I 15
Sephīrāh(ōth) I 4, 43-4; II 7-8, 39
   Talmudists call "Torah," the first I 5
   Seven Rays called the lower II 4
   same as the Elohīm II 42

Seven Eternities
   explained I 3, 8-9
Seven Rays, Logoi I 5, 14, 17, 23, 33, 43-4, 45-6; II 4, 12, 18, 28, 41
Sleep I 15, 23, 28, 35, 49-63; II 22
   analogy between, and pralaya I 10
   consciousness not active in I 53
   action of will during I 54-5
   explained I 58
   "unconscious cerebration" in I 60
   difference between, and death I 61
   black magic upon sleeper I 62
   nightmare during I 63
Son (see Father) I 34; II 13, 25, 27-8
   symbology of, of the immaculate Virgin II 6-7
Sons of the Fire, II 39-40
Space I 19, 23, 34-5, 43; II 6, 9-11, 17, 19, 22, 25-6, 33, 41, 45, 47
   is that Absolute All I 3-4
   why called feminine I 4
   seven layers of I 5
   ever was and ever will be I 10-13
   Parent and Cosmic I 30
Spirit I 31; II 25-6, 28, 30, 32, 40-1
   Voice, Word, and II 46-7
Subba Row I 6, 13-14, 35
Sun I 9, 39-40; II 4, 10, 13-14, 27, 29, 45-6
   relation of, to fire II 23-5
   heart of the II 25

Tetragrammaton II 7-8
   Logos becomes a II 8
Tetraktys II 4, 7
   astral plane lies between, and Tetragrammaton II 8
THAT I 34; II 28
   relation of "Eternal Parent" to I 5
Time (see Space) I 8-9, 19-20, 34-5, 43; II 6, 19, 33
   and Duration I 10-12; II 9-11
   an illusion I 13-16
"Torah," first Sephīrāh of Talmudists I 5
Tzirūph, process explained II 42

Vishnu I 44; II 18
   two meanings of I 31

War in Heaven
   and "churning of the ocean" II 20-1
Will I 27; II 3, 7, 33, 36
   in dreams I 54-5

Zero Point, State (see Laya) II 37
Zeruana-Akerne I 7